Edvard Munch

PRINTS

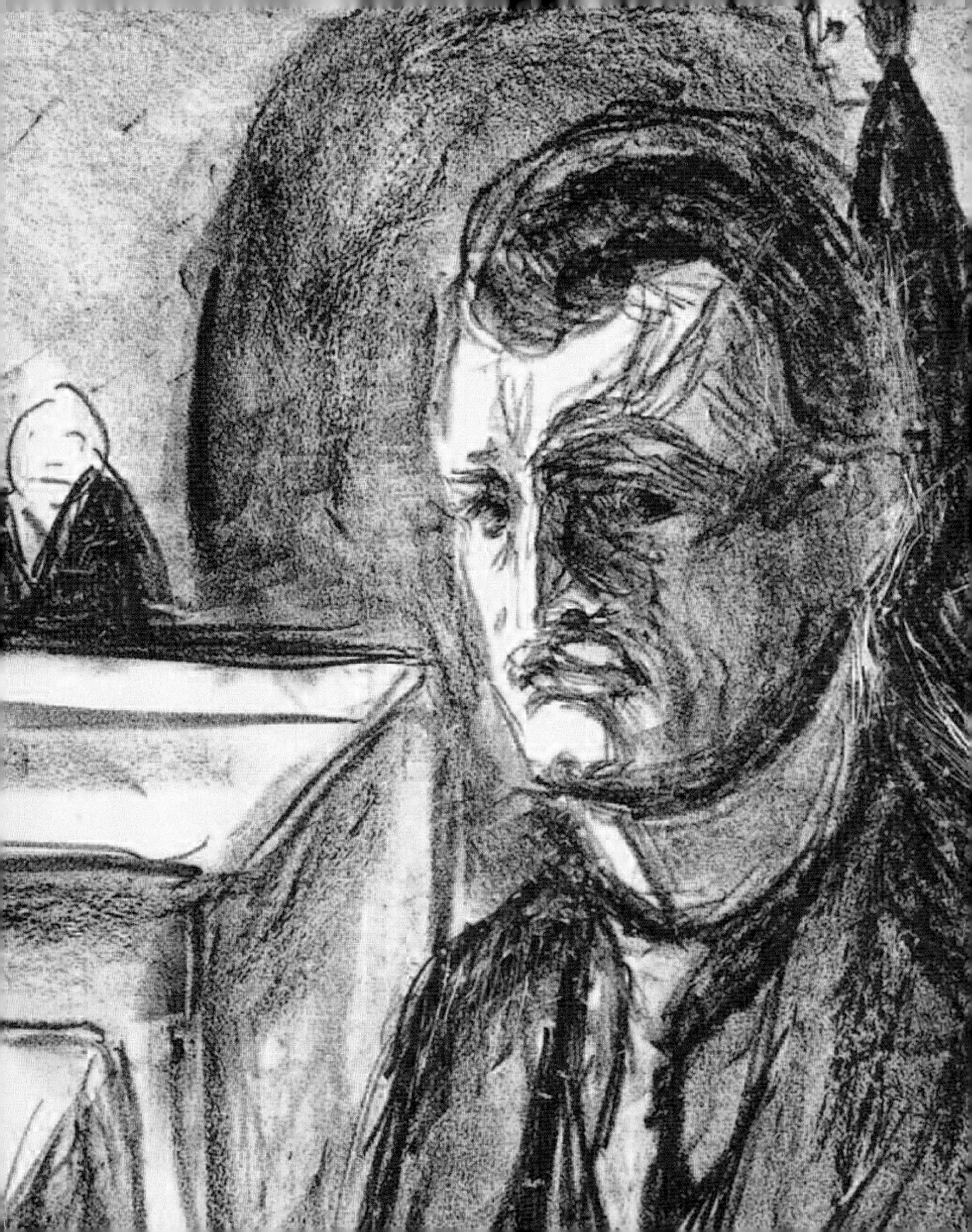

Edvard Munch
PRINTS

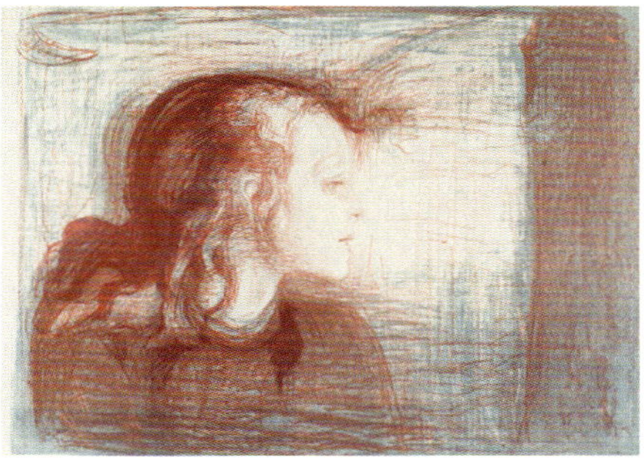

Philip Wilson Publishers
Hunterian Museum & Art Gallery,
University of Glasgow

This publication accompanies a loan exhibition from the Munch Museum, Oslo at the Hunterian Museum and Art Gallery, University of Glasgow from 12 June to 5 September 2009, and the National Gallery of Ireland, Dublin from 18 September to 6 December 2009.

www.hunterian.gla.ac.uk
www.nationalgallery.ie

First published in 2009 by
Philip Wilson Publishers Ltd.
109 Drysdale Street
The Timber Yard
London N1 6ND

www.philip-wilson.co.uk

Distributed throughout the world (excluding North America) by:
I.B. Tauris & Co. Ltd.
6 Salem Road
London W2 4BU

Distributed in North America by:
Palgrave Macmillan, a division of St Martin's Press
175 Fifth Avenue
New York NY 10010

ISBN: 978-0-85667-677-2 (paperback)

Edited by Matthew Hartley
Designed in Berthold Walbaum by Geoff Green Book Design, Cambridge
Printed in China by Everbest

Photographic Credits:
The photography of works at the Munch Museum was handled by Svein Andersen, Halvor Bjørngård, Jaro Hollan and Sidsel de Jong.

24: photography by Neil Miller, Glasgow University Photographic Department

Fig. 2 Max Klinger, *The Night*, from *On Death I*, Museumslandschaft Hessen Kassel, Graphische Sammlung

Fig. 5 Félix Vallotton, *A Th. Dostoieski*, Cabinet d'Estampes, Musées d'Art et d'Histoire, Geneva

Fig. 11 Jan Toorop, *Delft Salad Dressing*, Rijksmuseum, Amsterdam

Fig. 12 Paul Gauguin, *The Fresh Water is in Motion*, Albert Roullier Memorial Collection, 1926.27, The Art Institute of Chicago, photography © The Art Institute of Chicago

A Note on References throughout the Text
Munch's prints are referred to in this book in two ways. The exhibition that the book accompanies contains forty-one prints numbered 1–41. Prints not exhibited but mentioned in the text are accompanied by a number – in the form W. 236 – that refers to the standard catalogue, Gerd Woll, *Edvard Munch: The Complete Graphic Works* (London: Philip Wilson Publishers; New York: Harry Abrams, 2001). Throughout, reference is also made to Munch's manuscripts preserved in the Munch Museum, and these are referred to using the archive's numbers: T numbers (e.g. T 2770) refer to longer texts, often notebooks; N numbers (e.g. N 524) refer to shorter notes, often single loose sheets.

Acknowledgements

With thanks to all at the Munch Museum, especially the registrar who has handled this exhibition, Rikke Lundgreen. Anne Hodge and Fionnuala Croke of the National Gallery of Ireland, Dublin agreed with great enthusiasm to take the exhibition as a second venue, and we are very grateful to them, as we are to the gallery's registrar, Kim Smit. Particular thanks go to Pamela Robertson, senior curator at the Hunterian for her support of this project. Many others have helped in various ways, and we wish to record our gratitude in particular to John Denholm, Freek Heijbroek, Martin Hopkinson, Christiane Lukatis, Andrew Primrose, Christian Ruemelin, Martha Tedeschi and Gregor Weber.

We gratefully acknowledge the support of the Museums, Libraries and Archives Council (MLA), which administers the Government Indemnity Scheme. Thanks are due to Louise Adkin, manager of the scheme. We are also very grateful to Laura Ward-Ure, licensing executive, Design and Artists Copyright Society (DACS) for securing permission to reproduce works by Munch. Thanks are also due to the following for their help with research and location of photographs: Hannah Brocklehurst, National Gallery of Scotland; Ann Simpson, Scottish National Gallery of Modern Art; Ingrid Knauf, Museumslandschaft Hessen Kassel; Carina Greven, Rijksmuseum, Amsterdam; and Aimée Marshall, Art Institute of Chicago.

Financial Support

The exhibition and catalogue have been made possible by the support of a number of trusts and individuals, to whom we are very grateful. The University of Glasgow's Chancellor's Fund has been generous in its support of the Hunterian's exhibition programme 2009–10, and we are grateful for this. Thanks are also due to Mr Stein Iversen, head of press, information & cultural affairs of the Royal Norwegian Embassy, London, for supporting our publicity and marketing; to H.E. Ambassador Øyvind Nordsletten and First Secretary Signe Hjelde of the Royal Norwegian Embassy, Dublin; and to Milein Cosman and the trustees of the The Cosman Keller Art and Music Trust for their support towards photography and copyright fees. Our thanks also go to J. & J. Denholm Ltd., Glasgow, for their support of the exhibition. Additional support for the catalogue was received from Mrs Fiona Hope Johnstone and Mrs Patricia Johnstone Jackson, to whom we offer our warmest thanks.

A Note about the Typeface
Walbaum was cut in the early years of the nineteenth century. The font belongs to the classic tradition – vertical shading, unbracketed serifs and ranging figures. J.E. Walbaum (1768–1839) was a founder at Goslar and Weimar. This version is by Berthold, who purchased the matrices in 1919.

University of Glasgow | The Hunterian

Contents

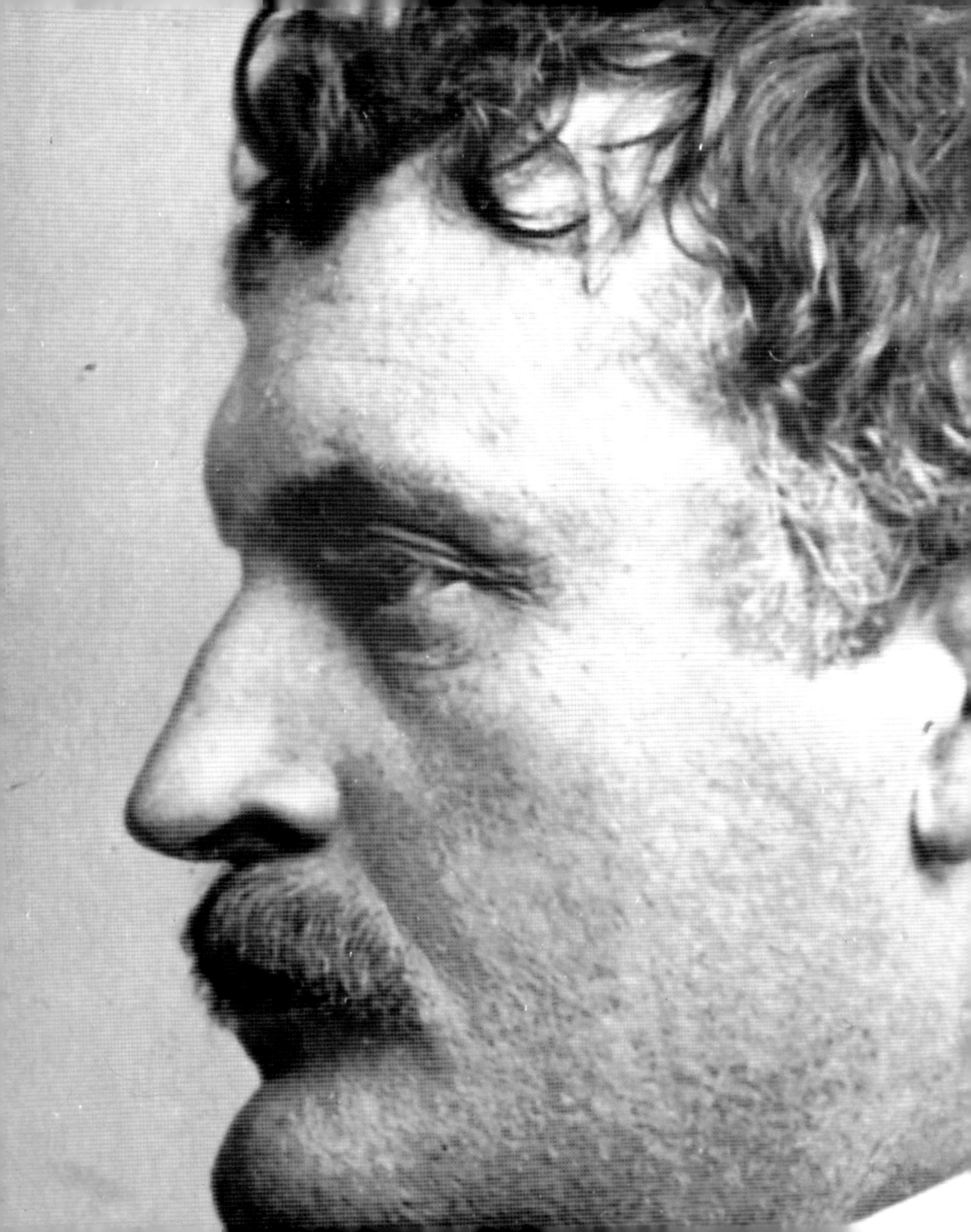

Foreword

The extraordinary strength of the Hunterian's art collections can be seen in the frequent requests received to lend works to temporary exhibitions in many of the world's greatest museums. Shows of Whistler and Mackintosh, for example, are rarely mounted without loans from our collections, though there are many other areas in which the University of Glasgow has surprising strengths. The idea of the present exhibition arose during our 2003 Whistler centenary exhibitions, which attracted a curator, Magne Bruteig, from the Munch Museum in Oslo to see Whistler's etchings. An exchange was suggested then that would allow us to show a selection of Munch's greatest prints and, in return, allow the Munch Museum to stage a Whistler exhibition selected from our own collections. The Hunterian has the most important collection of prints in Scotland. Even so, Munch's prints are notable by their rarity in British collections, and we are proud even to have two of them (to put this in context, the British Museum, which houses the UK's largest collection of modern prints, holds only nineteen of Munch's 748 graphic works). Without access to the unrivalled holdings of the Munch Museum in Oslo, no UK museum or gallery can mount an exhibition of this great Norwegian artist, whose prints represent some of the greatest images in twentieth-century art.

Following their showing in Glasgow, the prints will travel to the National Gallery of Ireland in Dublin, which has collaborated over a number of months with the Hunterian and the Munch Museum to bring this exciting exhibition to the Irish public.

Portrait of Munch in profile (detail), c.1910

Besides expressing my satisfaction that the University is participating in such an important cultural exchange, I would like to thank both the director of the Hunterian, Ewen Smith, and Ingebjørg Ydstie, director of the Munch Museum, for supporting the exchange of exhibitions, together with Raymond Keaveney, director of the National Gallery of Ireland in Dublin. This project has been overseen and the exhibition selected by Peter Black of the Hunterian, to whom our considerable thanks are also due.

SIR MUIR RUSSELL
Principal
University of Glasgow

Edvard Munch
PRINTS

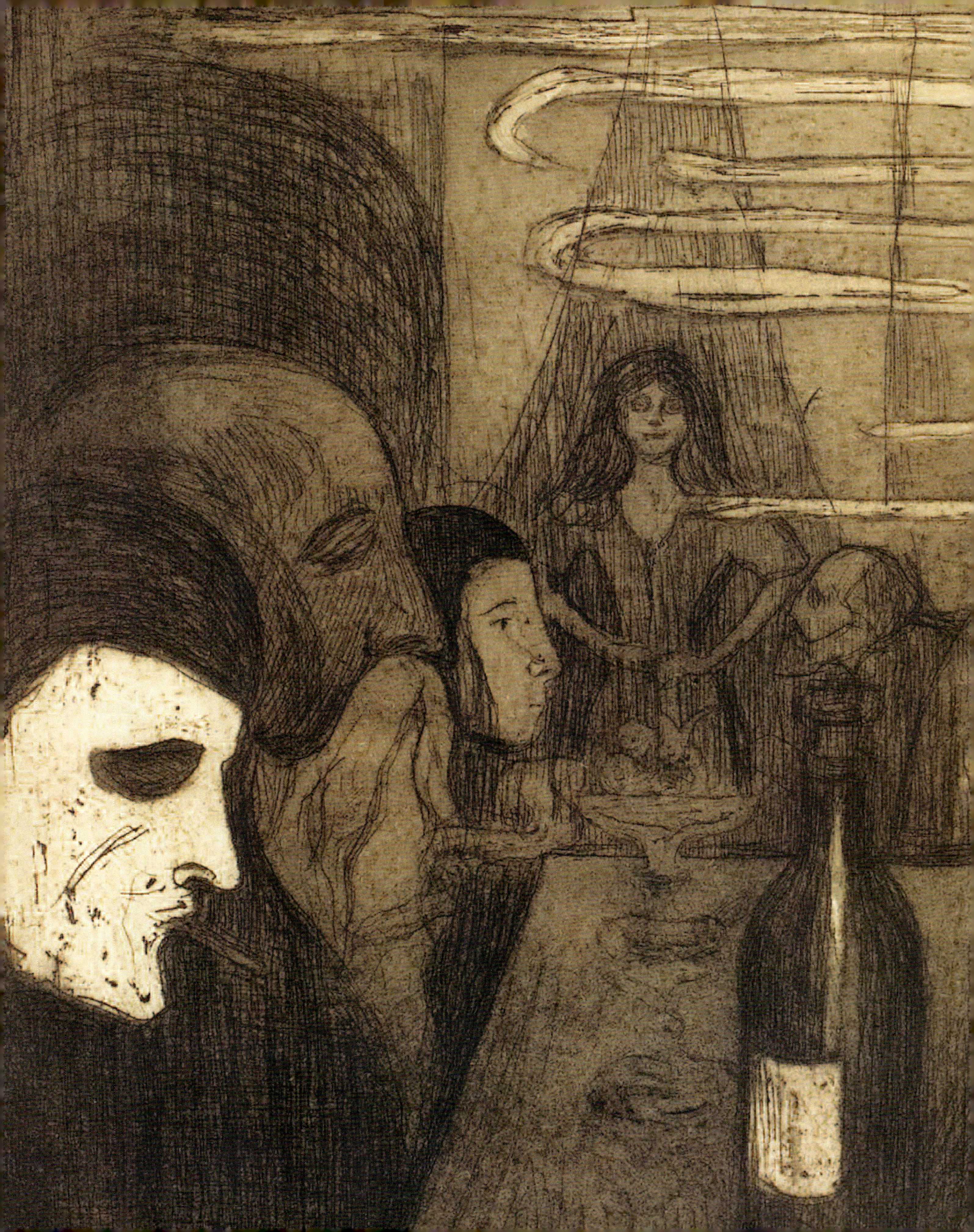

The Appreciation of Munch in Britain

PETER BLACK

Art and people
Hogarth painted
vice and Bohemians in
London. He was himself
a wealthy citizen who died happily
in the bosom of his family.

A Hogarth and a
Shakespeare.
The result of a kind of
British hypocrisy.

Edvard Munch

While the name of Edvard Munch is world famous, his work is not well known to British or Irish audiences, and this can be explained quite simply by the rarity of his paintings and prints in our museums and art galleries. Munch's art was hardly exhibited at all in Britain during his own lifetime, in dramatic contrast to his success exhibiting in mainland Europe. Munch, however, could not be accused of the same indifference. He was fond of quoting Shakespeare, whose plays were on his shelves alongside those of Ibsen (1828–1906) and Strindberg (1849–1912), and he thought of William Hogarth as a kindred spirit. His books also included works by Dickens and Aubrey Beardsley's influential illustrations to Oscar Wilde's *Salome,* which became a *cause célèbre* in the 1890s.

Kristiania Bohemians II (detail), 1895, etching, open bite and drypoint

Nevertheless, there is clearly some distance between Munch and his two British heroes named above in one of the many poetic texts that he wrote, often as literary versions of his images, but here more as a kind of prose poem. It happens that his contacts with Germany and France were closer and more heartfelt. Indeed, his influence extended throughout Germany and beyond, with exhibitions being organised as far afield as Prague (1905) and San Francisco (1915). Munch's international fame was achieved through an extraordinarily energetic campaign of exhibitions, which were mainly of his prints (listed in the chronology).

Munch's work was not always greeted with universal enthusiasm, however. His earliest paintings, for example, were sometimes ridiculed by the press, even in his home town of Kristiania (the name given to Oslo from the time of the great fire of 1624 until 1925), though he had a strong group of supporters there among the leading artists. In 1886 he exhibited in Kristiania's new annual Autumn Exhibition a painting called *The Sick Child*, which was a meditation on the death of his sister Sophie some eight years earlier. The painting received mixed criticism, some favourable, but also some doubtful and very negative – a fact that Munch's biographers have exaggerated– including the comment that it was '… no more than a rough sketch, half of which has been scraped away … a miscarriage'.[1] It was not long, however, before *The Sick Child* was rehabilitated. The image furnished the subject for a lithograph now recognised as one of Munch's greatest prints (16), and by 1912, the year of the international Sonderbund Exhibition of 'New Painting' in Cologne, it was understood to be one of the crucial first works of the movement newly christened 'Expressionism'. In fact, this rehabilitation was so complete that in 1931 Oslo's National Gallery managed to exchange its second version of the painting, given in 1909 by the collector Olaf Schou, for the original, which was then owned by Harold Nørregaard.[2] Munch was one of two living artists given a substantial showing at Cologne – the other was Picasso – and his was the largest section dedicated to any artist after the retrospective sections dedicated to Cézanne, Van Gogh and Gauguin.

1 *Death and the Woman*
1894, drypoint
Munch and his writer friends were preoccupied with the theme of love and death. Munch once remarked that this plate was intended as a frontispiece to a book by his friends August Strindberg and Stanlislaw Przybyszewski, both of whom held unconventional views about relationships between the sexes. The decorative border alludes symbolically to the image, a device known to Munch from Max Klinger's etchings. The motifs of sperm and foetuses were soon also incorporated in the border of Munch's most controversial lithograph, *Madonna* (10).

1 Andreas Aubert, 'Kunstnernes 5te Høstudstilling', *Morgenbladet*, 569, 9 November 1886, 1, quoted in Reinhold Heller, *Munch, His Life and Work* (London: John Murray, 1984), 36.

2 Gerd Woll, *Edvard Munch: The Complete Paintings* (London: Thames & Hudson, 2009) cat. 130, 146.

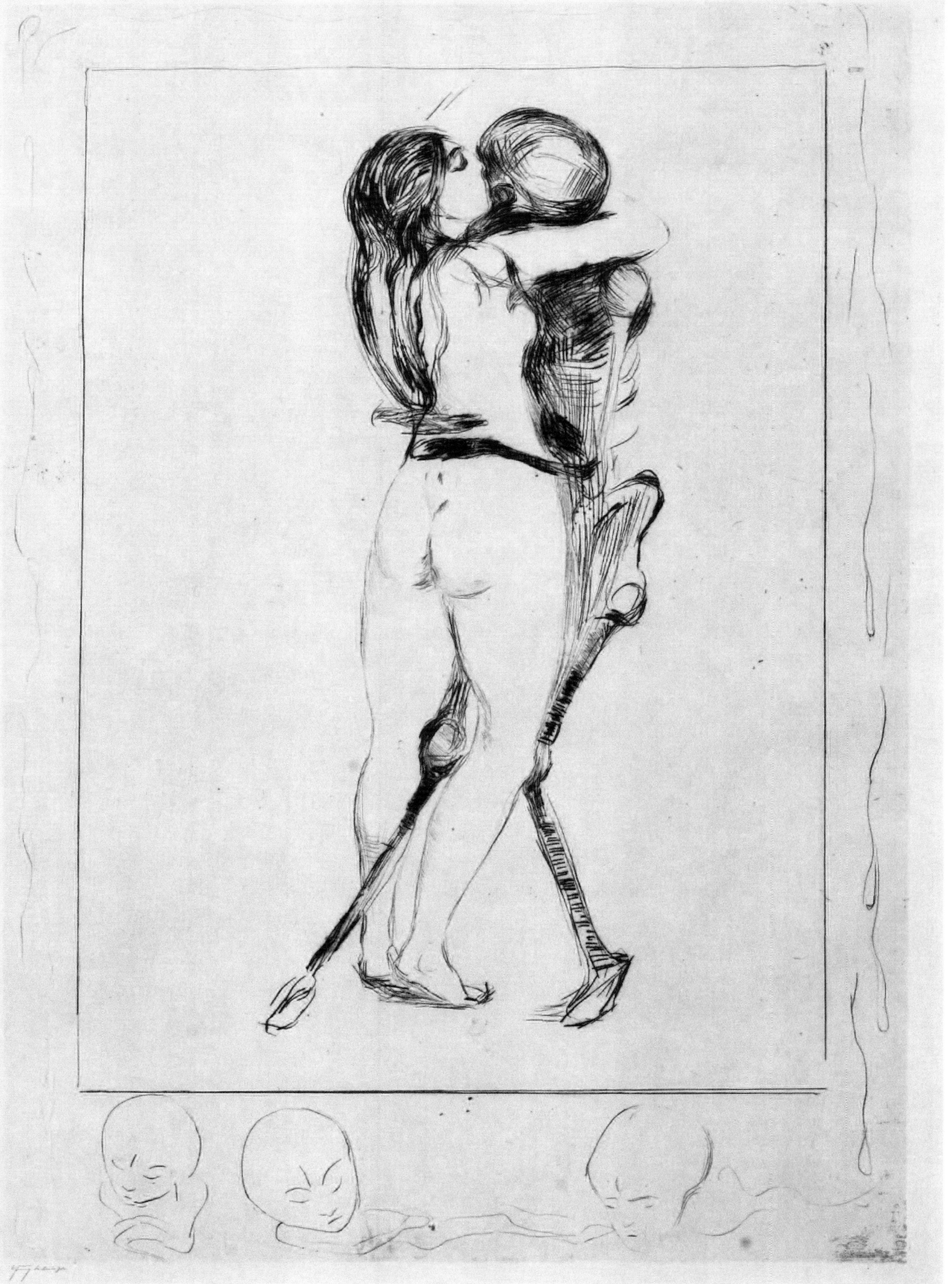

While in mainland Europe Munch achieved extraordinary fame, no international exhibitions promoted German or Scandinavian painting in Britain. Instead, due to the distinctly pro-Parisian aesthetics instilled by important early-twentieth-century exhibition organisers such as Roger Fry, but also because of the habitual British hostility towards Germanic culture following World War I, Munch would remain known only to a few until the late twentieth century, despite having been recognised in Germany as one of the 'fathers of Expressionism'. The contrast is great. Indeed, the collector Gustav Schiefler (1857–1935), writing the foreword to his complete catalogue of Munch's prints in Hamburg in 1927, went so far as to claim that Munch had '... achieved in life what happens with most great figures only after they die – to become a sort of mythological personage'.[3]

Although widespread appreciation of Munch came much later in the British Isles than in Europe, there were enlightened individuals who promoted his work, even before World War II. Herbert Read – who was a follower of Nietzsche and, from early on, familiar with modern European painting from works in Michael Sadler's collection in Leeds – lectured on Munch in Edinburgh in 1931 during the show organised by the Society of Scottish Artists. In stark contrast to Read's endorsement of the work, however, local reactions to the adventurous loan exhibition of fifteen paintings challenged even those that met the artist's work in Kristiania in 1886 for insularity. Read later wrote an introduction for Munch's show at the London Gallery in 1936, after which the artist presented the British Museum with its first two prints (there are currently nineteen housed there). After World War II, the critic J.P. Hodin, born in Prague, educated in Sweden, and an emigré from Germany in 1945, was one of very few voices that spoke in favour of central European art. Hodin's book on Munch, based on conversations with the artist in Prague in 1936 and again in Norway in 1938, was published in German in Stockholm in 1948, and in 1972 he published a shorter monograph in English.[4]

The exhibition at the Tate Gallery in 1950, in which a hundred prints were shown, can be regarded as the beginning of a general appreciation of Munch's work in Britain, and over the following

2 *The Day After*
1894, drypoint
This print of a young woman sleeping off a night of excess was included in 1895 in the portfolio of eight drypoints published by Julius Meier-Graefe (1867–1935). Meier-Graefe observed in the accompanying booklet that the images 'mirror some of Munch's most important concerns: the psyche of man and the perception he projects onto the physical world' (Prelinger, 1983, 16). The other published prints were: *The Girl at the Window* (W. 5), *The Sick Child* (W. 7), *Tête-à-tête* (W. 9), *Two Human Beings. The Lonely Ones* (W. 13), *Kristiania Bohemians I* (W. 15), *Moonlight. Night in St Cloud* (6) and *Portrait (Dr Max Asch)* (W. 25).

3 Quoted by Sigrid Achenbach in *Edvard Munch, Die Graphik im Berliner Kupferstichkabinett* (Berlin: G+H Verlag, 2003), 12.

4 J.P. Hodin, *Edvard Munch* (London: Thames & Hudson, 1972).

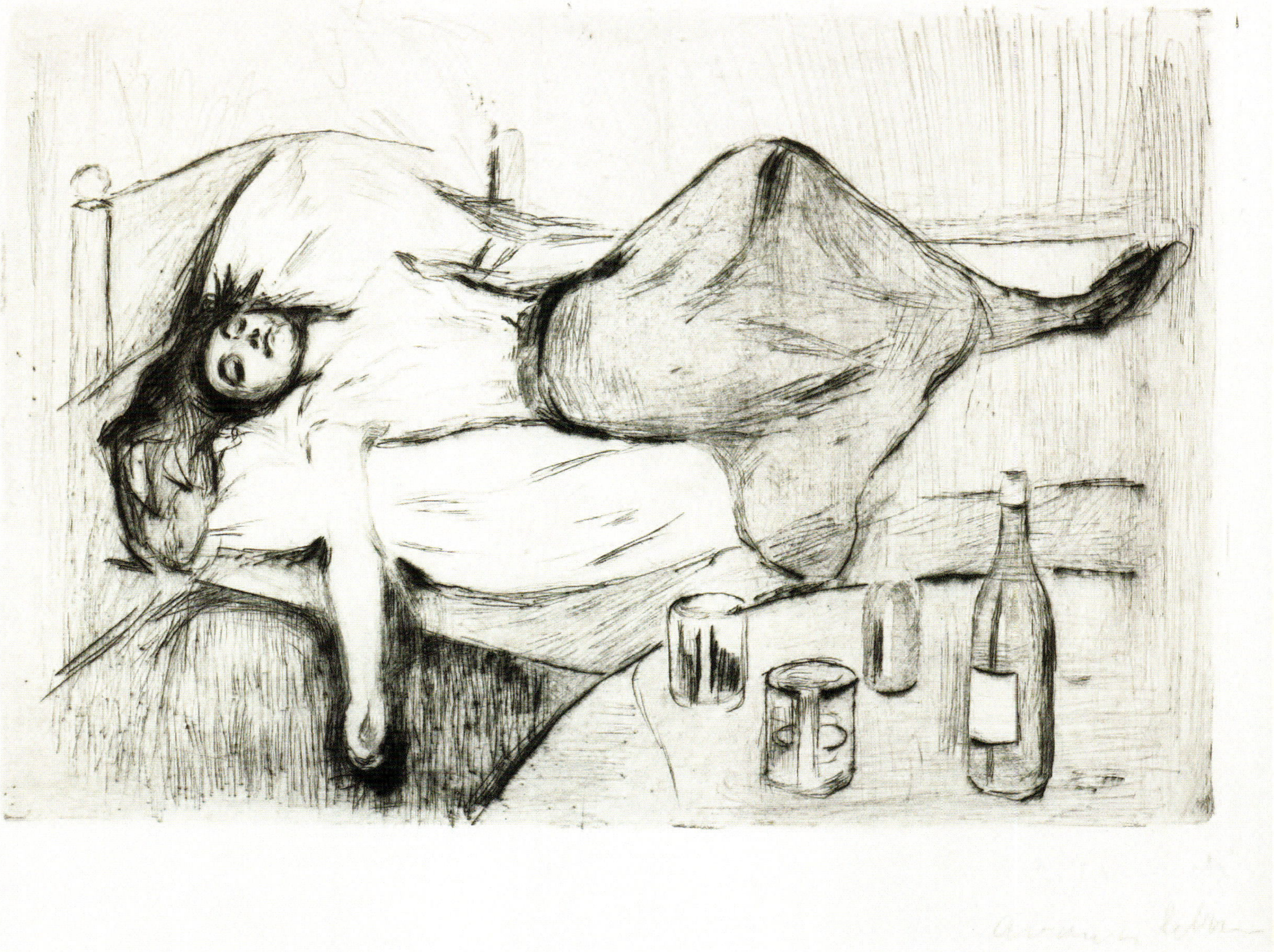

3 *Madonna*, 1894, drypoint

In this first version of one of Munch's most famous subjects, the sexual imagery reflects the interests and unconventional thinking of Munch's Bohemian friends, notably Hans Jaeger in Kristiania and Stanislaw Przybyszewski (12), then in Berlin, who encouraged Munch's focus on man's psyche and on making an account of his own life. Munch distanced himself from the free love advocated by Jaeger, but regarded the moment in which life is created as 'holy'. Several versions of this ecstatic woman figure were made before the larger, more famous print *Madonna* (10).

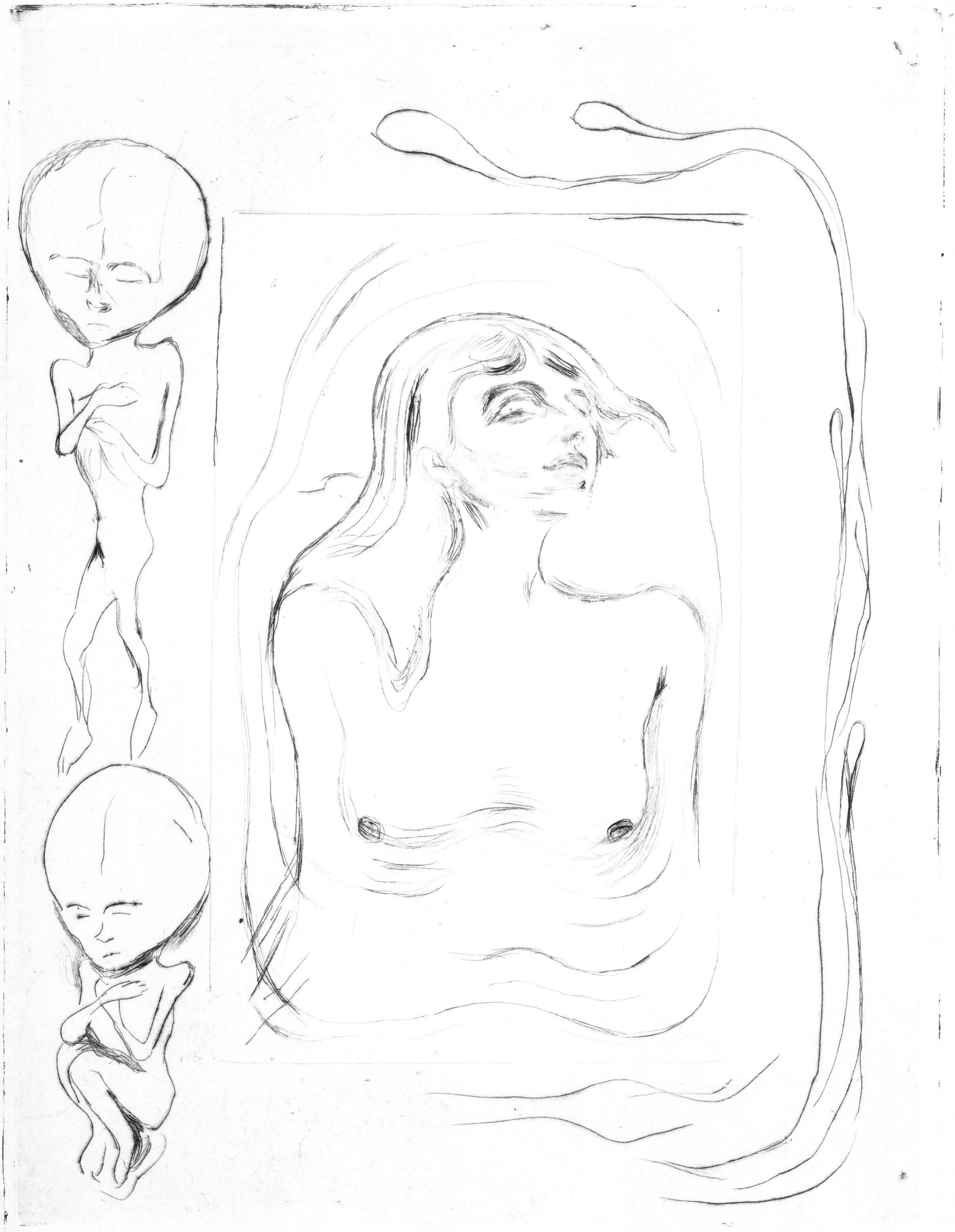

4 *Summer Night. The Voice*, 1894, etching, open bite and drypoint

It has been shown that the beautiful young woman who stares up at the artist on the shore at Åsgårdstrand resembles Milly Thaulow. Memories of an early love affair haunted Munch for years. Reinhold Heller (1984, 19) states that Milly (Munch's 'Mrs Heiberg') was 'the woman who totally transformed his attitude towards life', and quotes Munch: 'What a deep mark she has made on my mind, so deep that no other image can ever totally drive it away. Was it because she was so much prettier than the others? No, I do not even know that she was pretty; her mouth was large' (T.2770, c.1890).

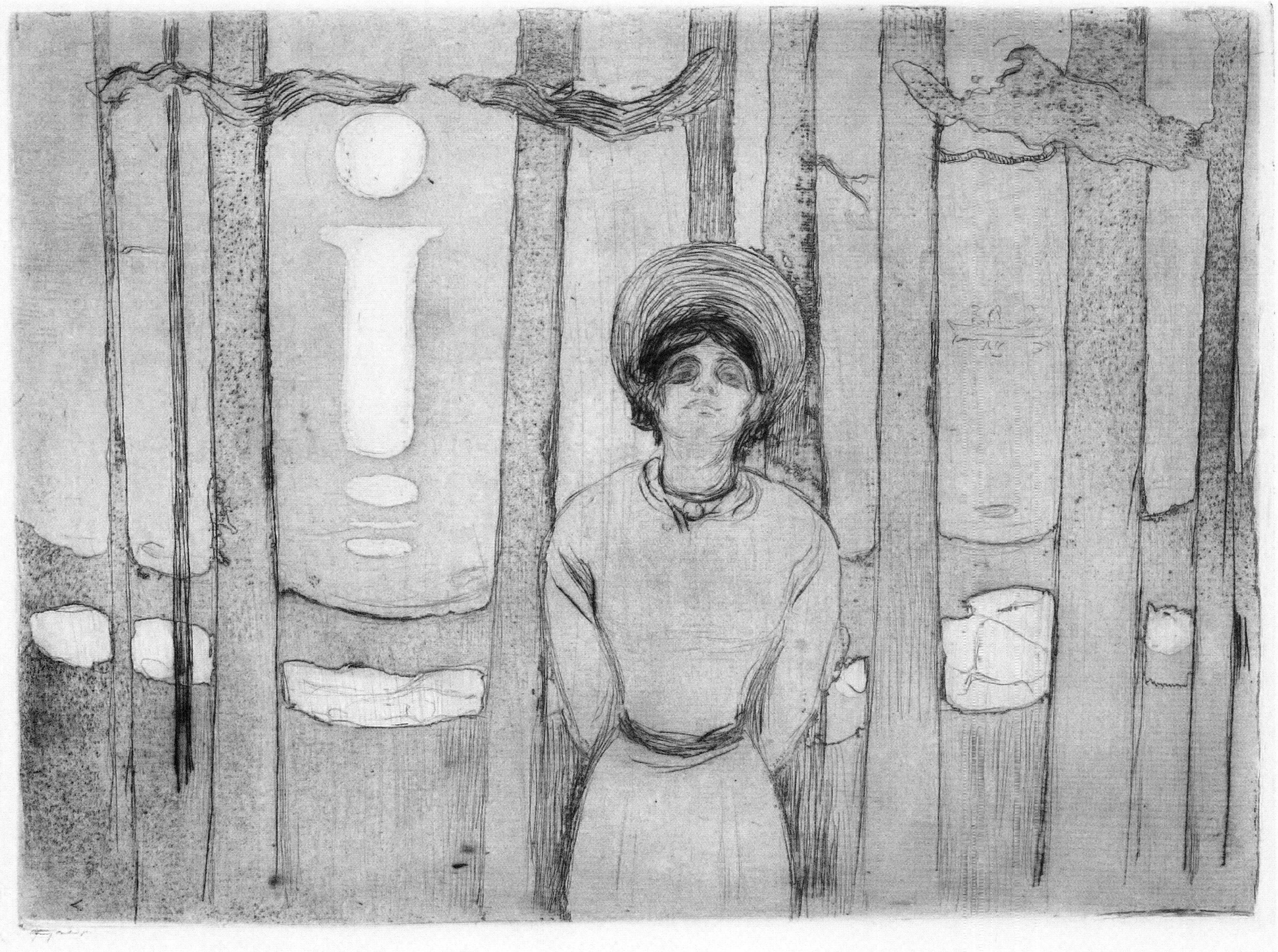

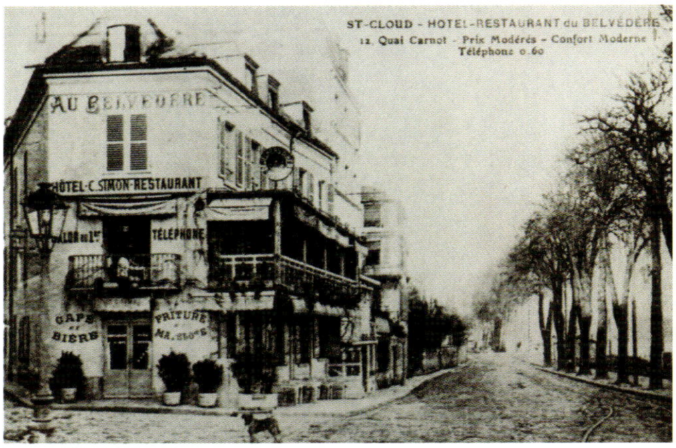

Fig. 1 Postcard view of Hotel du Belvédère, St Cloud, where Munch stayed as a student in Paris, 1890–92, B 3584 (F)

decades there have been regular loan shows, which, in the main part, have been selections from the paintings. The process of bringing Munch to the public around the world today is the work of the scholars at the Munch Museum in Oslo. They have generously supported exhibitions that have come to Britain, and their own work has resulted in exemplary studies, such as the recent Munch Becoming Munch exhibition (2008–09), which was about the period immediately before Munch made his first prints and included a remarkable reconstruction of his scandalous Verein Berliner Künstler exhibition of 1892.

Munch might not have fared as well in his own lifetime as he did, and he might not have been honoured at Cologne in 1912, had he not made the impressive body of prints that are the focus of this book. As a teenager, Munch learned about lithography from a relative – Karl Frederik Diriks (1814–95) – who encouraged the Munch family to draw humorous sketches on transfer paper. Indeed, influenced by Diriks, Munch printed a set of *Pen Drawings* at Christmas 1882, although this did not immediately lead to the making of further lithographs.[5]

5 *Kristiania Bohemians II,* 1895, etching, open bite and drypoint

Among Munch's earliest prints made in Berlin are two interiors that recall his youth in Kristiania in the 1880s, and which are named after the 1885 novel of his friend Hans Jaeger, *From the Kristiania Bohemians* (*Fra Kristiania Bohêmen*). The first version (W. 15) was included in the Meier-Graefe portfolio. In this, the second version, the writers and painters of Munch's circle can all be identified. The men are arranged around the magnetic figure of Oda Krohg, wife of the painter. They are (left to right): Munch, Christian Krohg, Jappe Nilssen, Oda Krohg, Hans Jaeger, Gunnar Heiberg and Jørgen Engelhardt.

The circle of artists with whom Munch rented a studio in 1882, in the Pultosten building, were painters and not graphic artists. In fact, there were no institutions that promoted printmaking in Kristiania until many years after their institution in Paris (Société des Acquafortistes, 1862) and London (The Society of Painter-Etchers, 1880). Frances Carey identifies some important events in Norwegian printmaking that occurred around 1900, but which came too late to create the climate in which an artist like Munch could have taken up printmaking seriously. Carey mentions the funding of a trip to Berlin in 1898 for Johan Nordhagen (1856–1956) to study printmaking with Karl Köpping (1848–1914) '... so that he could effectively run the first engraving class at the School of Arts and

5 The sketches are described in Gerd Woll, *Edvard Munch: The Complete Graphic Works* (London: Philip Wilson Publishers; New York: Harry Abrams, 2001), Appendix 1, 438–39.

6 Frances Carey, *Modern Scandinavian Prints* (London: British Museum Publications, 1997), 14–15.

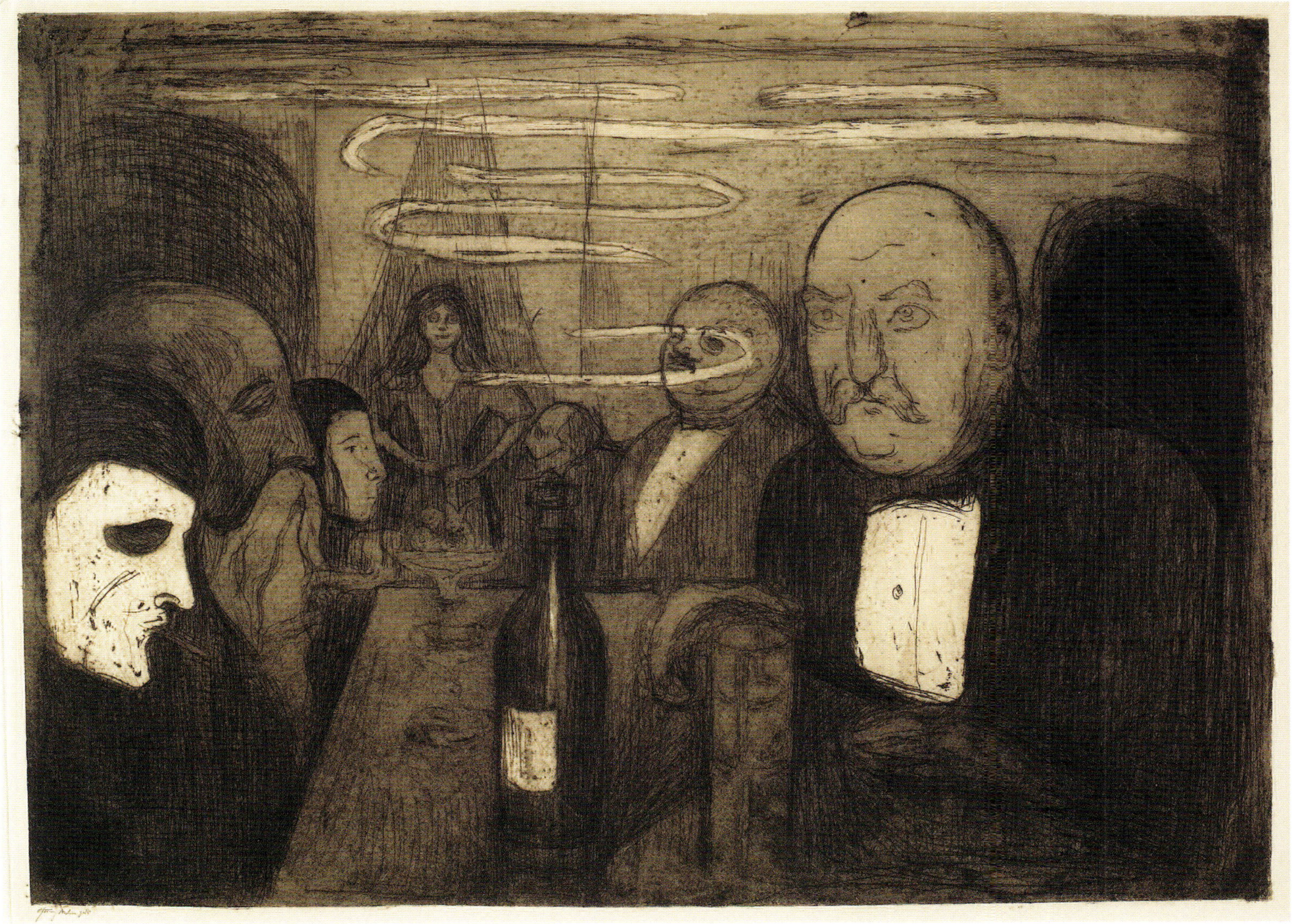

6 *Moonlight. Night in St Cloud*, 1895, drypoint

The image is one on which Munch worked intensively during his time in Paris between 1889 and 1892 (a related painting was included in the 1892 Verein Berliner Künstler exhibition). In 1890 Munch moved to the riverside suburb of St Cloud with a Danish poet, Emanuel Goldstein (1862–1921). It was in Paris that Munch had heard the news of his father's death, to which the image refers symbolically, principally through the figure of the depressed man seated by the window. Goldstein modelled for this figure, but it most likely represents Munch himself. The print was included in the Meier-Graefe portfolio.

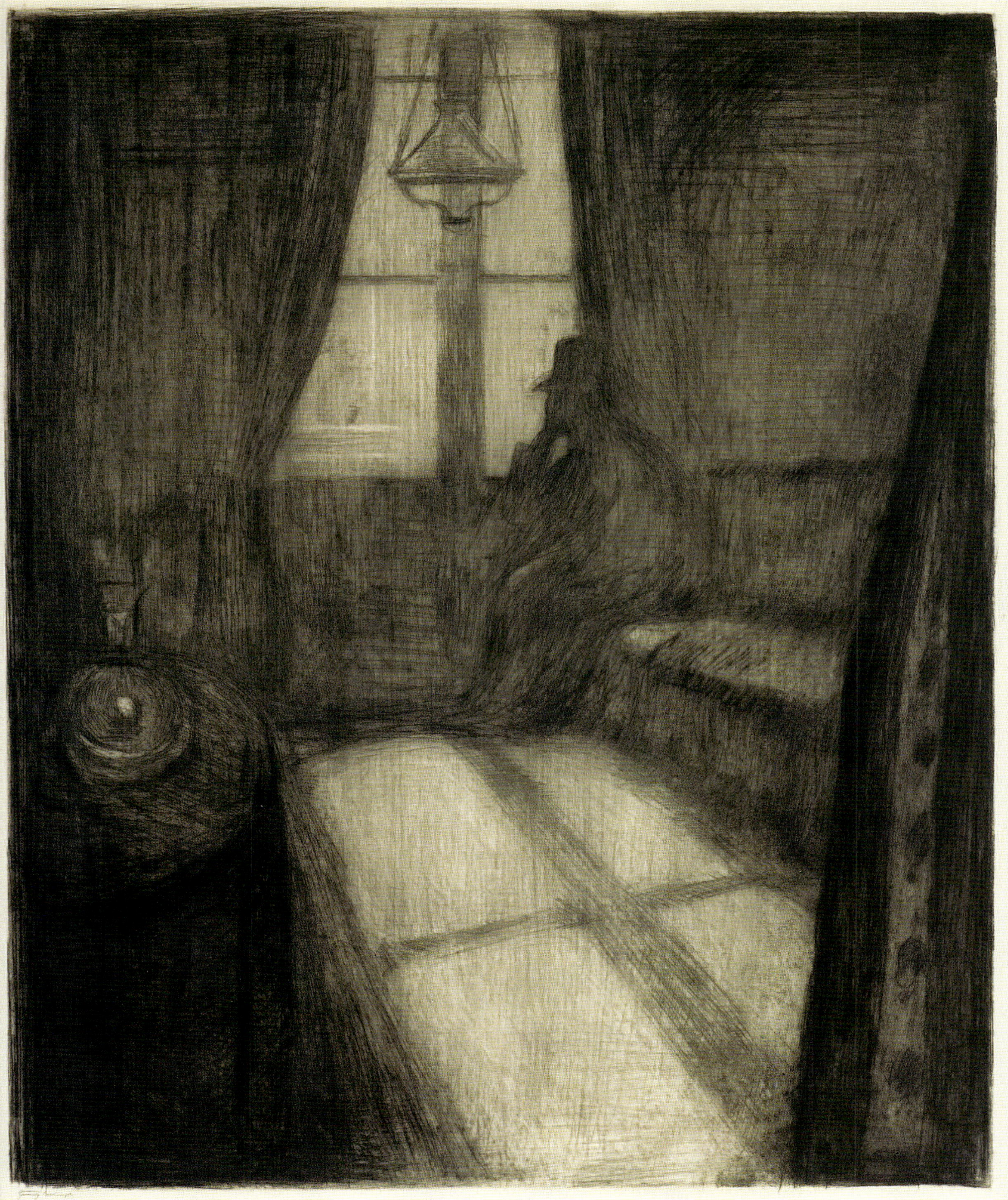

Crafts in Oslo.'[6] Furthermore, Oslo acquired its Academy of Fine Arts only in 1909, after full independence, and the first commercial organisation set up to promote only prints, Norske Grafikere, was not founded until 1919, and then Munch was one of those who brought it into being, along with Erik Werenskiold (1855–1938) and Harald Sohlberg (1869–1935).

Among the few Norwegian artists of Munch's circle who made prints was Fritz Thaulow (1847–1906), who encouraged Munch and supported him financially as a young man. Thaulow's commercially successful colour etchings were stimulated by the different market conditions that prevailed outside Scandinavia – in Paris and the United States during the 1890s and early 1900s. Writing home from Paris in September 1896, Munch expressed his need to make prints, but spoke also of the barrier posed by their unfamiliarity back in Norway: 'I must have money for my work, which I believe may come to be of importance – at least in initiating an art form that is not known at home, namely printmaking.'[7]

Munch's Berlin exhibition of 1892, which was closed because of the shock caused by his pictures, was advertised with a press-release stating that the artist's aim was to create 'Ibsen'sche Stimmungsbilder' – mood pictures in the Ibsen style. Munch naturally craved the international attention that the great Norwegian playwright found outside Scandinavia, and so it was also natural for him to turn his attention to the publication of prints, which were works of art analogous to the publications that had spread Ibsen's fame. This seemed all the more clear, no doubt, as looking at recently published artists' prints was necessary for anyone in Kristiania who wanted to see what famous artists in Dresden or Paris were producing.

From about 1880 onwards until the financial collapse of 1929, artistic careers could be built on the creation of prints alone. Market conditions and tastes had changed, with the result that the artist was no longer dependent on the translation of a painting into print as a reproduction. By the 1850s, which was a low point for the production of original prints everywhere, engraved reproductions were a necessary marketing tool for successful painters, and producing them meant buying the skills and time

7 *Woman II (The Woman in Three Stages)*, 1895, drypoint, etching and open bite

Woman II is a Symbolist work that presents woman as a puzzling three-formed being: first staring innocently across the sea as a pubescent girl, then as a rapturous sexual being, and finally as the disappointed widow who turns away from the ocean. In Berlin, Munch read Gunnar Heiberg's play *The Balcony* (1894), and quoted from it for the catalogue entry for a related painting called *The Sphinx*: 'All others are one. You are a thousand' (Lathe, 1978, 19–20). The line is spoken by one of the lovers of Heiberg's character Julia, a woman of Munch's middle, fertile stage.

7 Quoted by Bente Torjusen in 'The Mirror' in Robert Rosenblum, Arne Eggum et al., *Edvard Munch: Images & Symbols* (Washington, D.C.: National Gallery of Art, 1978), 185.

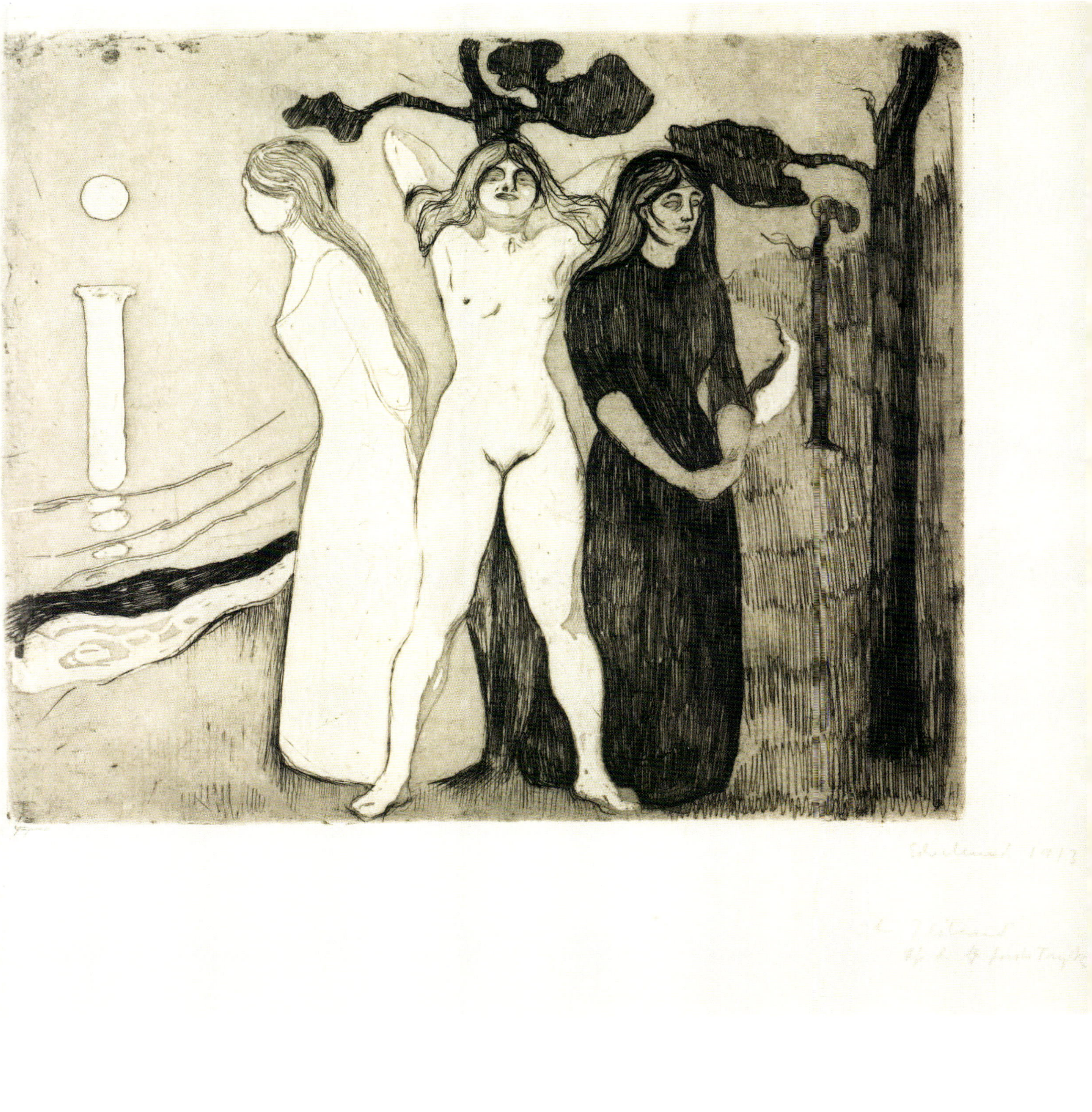

of professional printmakers. This could work economically only with the investment of a wealthy print publisher, however, and even then only for pictures with mass appeal. Whistler is the most famous example in London of an artist who rejected the engraved reproduction to market his own prints and turned his 'copper into gold', printing his way out of bankruptcy during the 1880s. Munch also seems to have had an instinctive sense of the advantages obtainable from producing his own prints, and the decade 1895–1905 saw him feverishly create a graphic oeuvre to satisfy his almost religious need of exporting his imagery to a larger, international audience.

Munch started late as a printmaker, and one extraordinary aspect of his prints is that we see no 'early' or student work: when he took up a copper plate and a drypoint needle in 1894, his imagery was ready formed. In the judgment of Curt Glaser (1879–1943), who wrote an important book on Munch in 1917 and was responsible, as keeper of the Berlin Kupferstichkabinett, for the formation of the greatest collection of Munch's prints in Germany, Munch speaks in his earliest prints with the mature voice of the first Expressionist artist: 'Von der ersten Radierung an spricht der reife Künstler'.[8]

Although some will undoubtedly remember the 1972 Arts Council travelling exhibition Edvard Munch: The Graphic Work, which was shown at Kelvingrove Art Gallery and Museum in Glasgow, at the Walker Art Gallery, Liverpool and elsewhere, there are inevitably several generations who have not had an opportunity to see Munch's prints. The Hunterian Art Gallery has strong holdings of late nineteenth- and early twentieth-century prints, including works by some of Munch's contemporaries acquired by Whistler in Paris in the 1890s. Like other museums in Britain, however, we have very little by Munch. It is the aim of this exhibition not only to introduce Munch's prints to those who have not had opportunities to see them, but also to consolidate the reputation of a major European artist whose work remains surprisingly little known in Britain.

8 *Self-Portrait*, 1895, lithograph
This is one of the greatest self-portrait prints. Munch's head emerges from the rich black lithographic wash like a Symbolist apparition conjured up by Odilon Redon; it might also have been influenced by Vallotton's woodcut portraits of Dostoiewski (fig. 5) or *E.A. Poe* (1894). The black behind the artist's image symbolises a memorial tablet. Munch's face floats between his epitaph above and the artist's skeletal arm below. Munch wrote to Jens Thiis: 'The greatest colour is black, the most essential colour. It is the *tabula rasa* for pure expression. Nothing prostitutes it' (Draft, undated, Munch Museum).

8 Curt Glaser, *Edvard Munch* (Berlin: Bruno Cassirer, 1917), 86. On Glaser see Sigrid Achenbach, *Edvard Munch: Die Graphik im Berliner Kupferstichkabinett* (Berlin: G+H Verlag, 2003), 9–15.

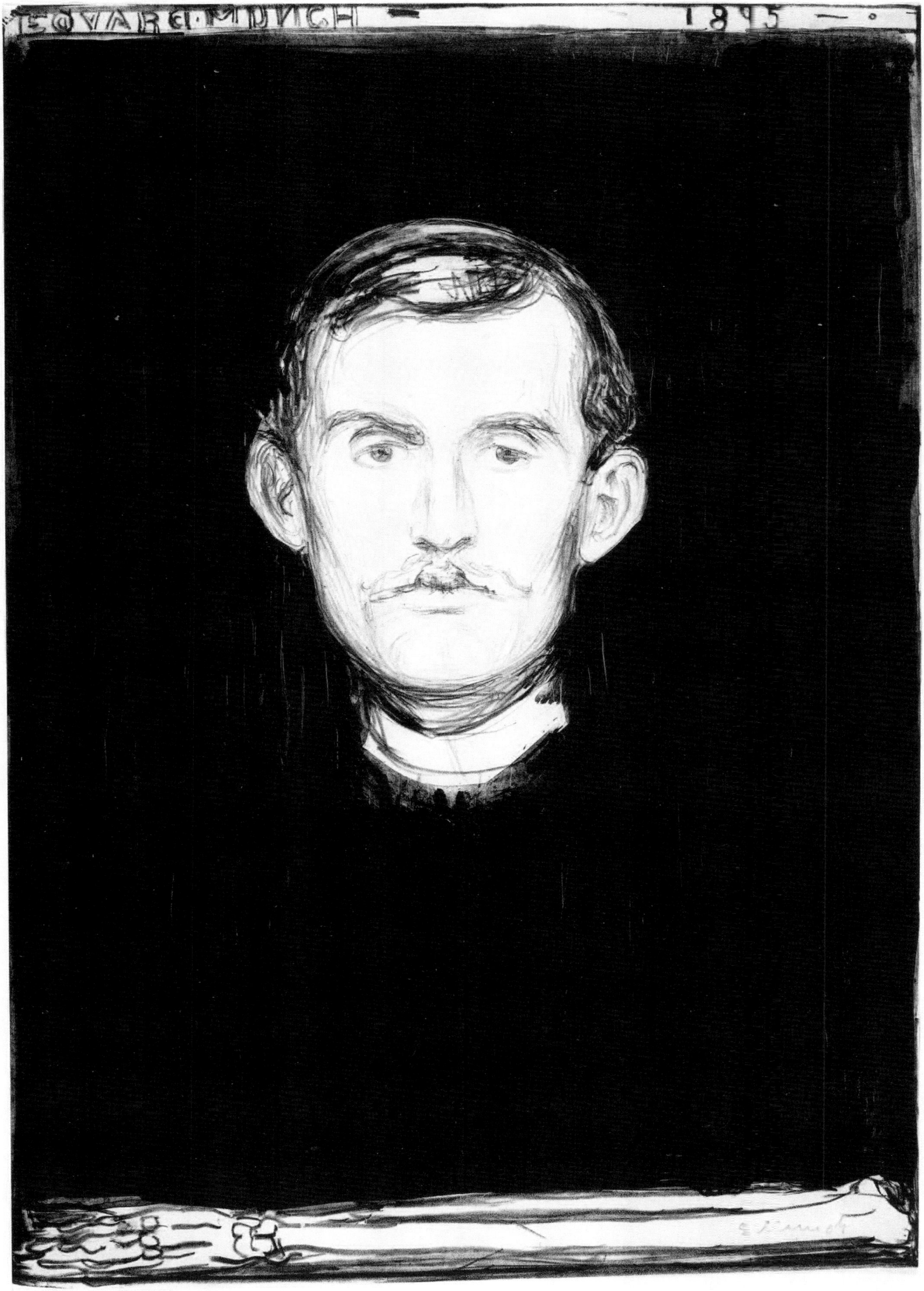
EDVARD·MUNCH — 1895 —

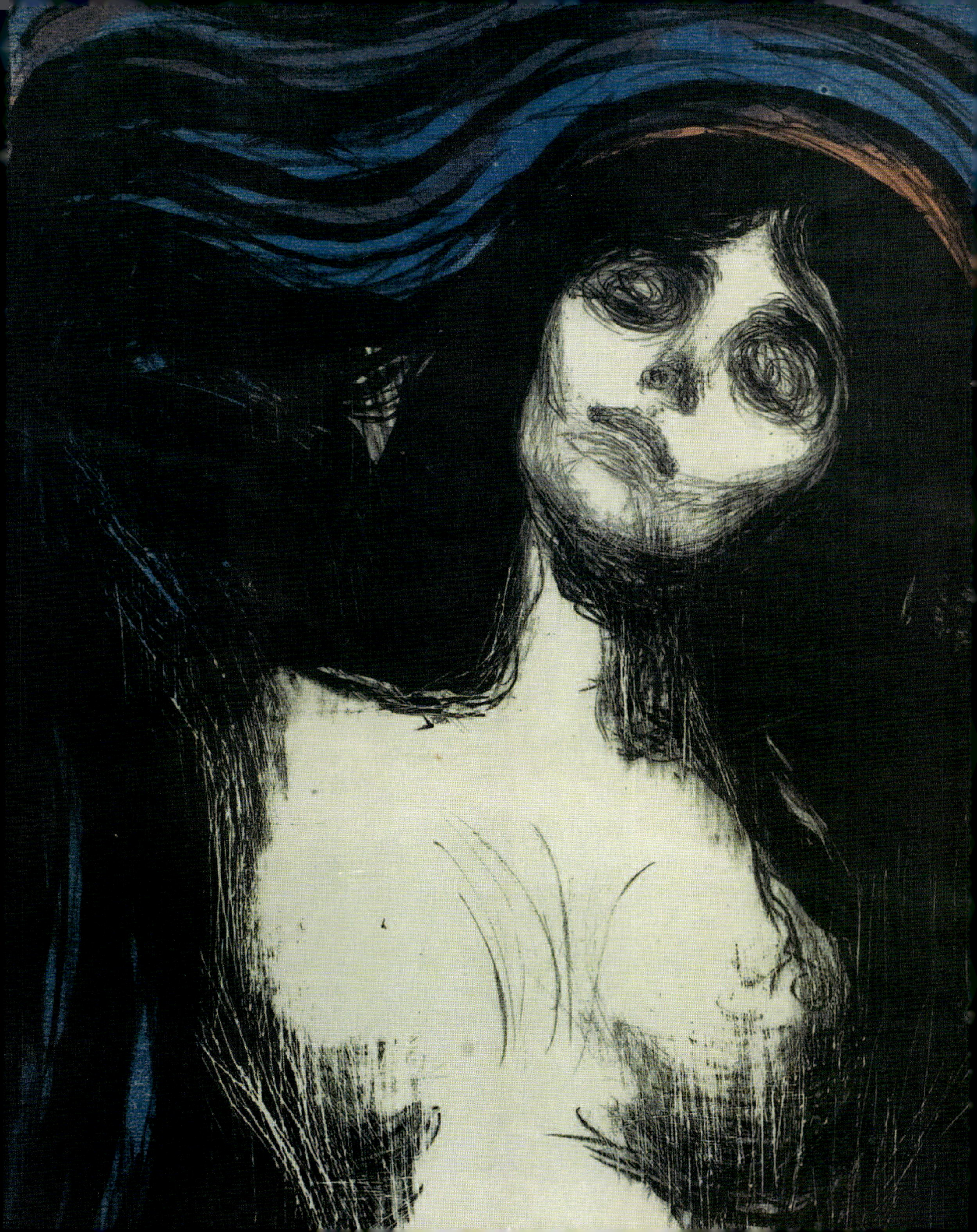

Visual Poetry: An Account of Munch's Prints, 1894–1930

MAGNE BRUTEIG

When Munch took up printmaking in 1894, the time was ripe. He was well informed of the situation in Paris, where lithographic posters by Jules Chéret and Henri de Toulouse-Lautrec were bringing colour to the city, and art magazines were printing graphic works by virtually all well-known painters and sculptors, such as Rodin, Redon, Degas, Manet, Renoir, Cassatt, Vallotton and Pissarro. Large annual graphic exhibitions were also organised there, and portfolios of original graphic art works appeared on the market.

Munch, however, started his graphic career in Berlin, where there were also a number of influential artists who had taken up the drypoint needle and the lithographic crayon. Max Klinger (1857–1920) had been producing important portfolios of etchings since 1880, such as *Eva and the Future* (1880), *A Glove* (1881) and *A Love Affair* (1887). Some of these Munch may have already seen in Kristiania, where his 'mentor', an established painter Christian Krohg (1852–1925), owned an extensive collection of prints by his old fellow-student Klinger. It was also around the time Munch bought his first copper plates that Klinger released his *Brahms-phantasy* portfolio. In addition to his prints, Klinger wrote an essay in 1891 entitled *Painting and Drawing* , which formed the theoretical basis for the revival of the graphic arts in Germany. In it he maintained that '... intaglio prints are through their distinctive character predetermined to produce mental and imaginative ideas.' Another motivating influence was Max Liebermann (1847–1935), who had been making prints since 1887 and became the leading

Madonna (detail), 1895/1902, lithograph

Fig. 2 Max Klinger, *The Night*, from *On Death I*, 1882–85, etching, Museumslandschaft Hessen Kassel, Graphische Sammlung

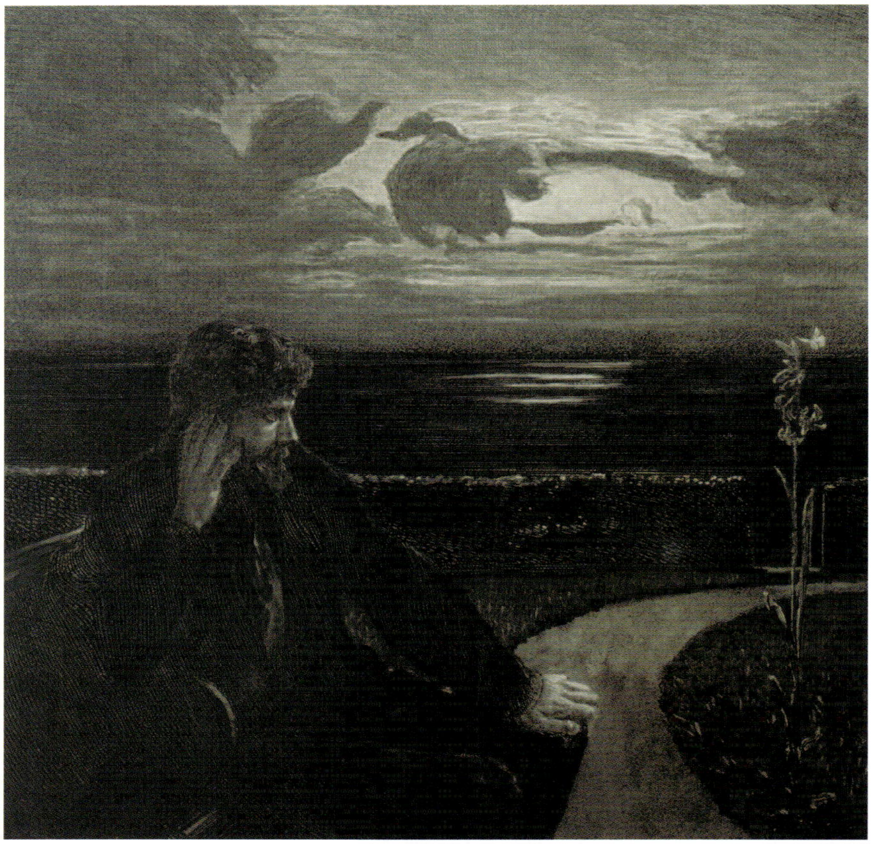

9 *The Scream*, 1895, lithograph
The fame of Munch's first painted version of *The Scream* (1893) has obscured the Parisian literary context in which this lithograph was promoted. Its boldness prompted Munch's friend Przybyszewski to comment: 'There is something dreadful and macrocosmic in that picture' (Hodin, 1972, 81). Munch and his friend Emanuel Goldstein were painting and writing pieces designed to create 'vibrations of feeling in the reader' (Lathe, 1979, 9). Arne Eggum states that *The Scream* was made in response to Schopenhauer, whose *Philosophy of Art* stated that 'the limit of the power of expression of a work of art was its inability to reproduce a scream, "das Geschrei", precisely the title which Munch was to give his motif' (Eggum, 1998, 34).

painter-printmaker in Berlin during the 1890s. Numerous other artists, such as Karl Stauffer-Bern (1857–1891), Ernst Moritz Geyger (1861–1941) and Käthe Kollwitz (1867–1945), were active printmakers, and their work may have influenced Munch's decision to try out this artistic medium.

However, around the table at Zum Schwarzen Ferkel, the Berlin tavern that became an avant-garde melting pot during the 1890s, there were more poets, writers and playwrights than artists. August Strindberg and Stanislaw Przybyszewski, in particular, were important partners for Munch in his search for artistic identity. They may not have directly urged Munch to make prints, but they, and other artists producing literature, made their art known to the public by means of printing. This cannot have been lost on Munch, for the question of how one could reach an audience was particularly important for him, regarding himself as an artist with a mission.

The Schwarzen Ferkel circle also included, on its periphery, a group of writers and art historians who were planning the launch of a new periodical called *Pan*, which encompassed modern art and literature. Among these, the board chairman Eberhardt von

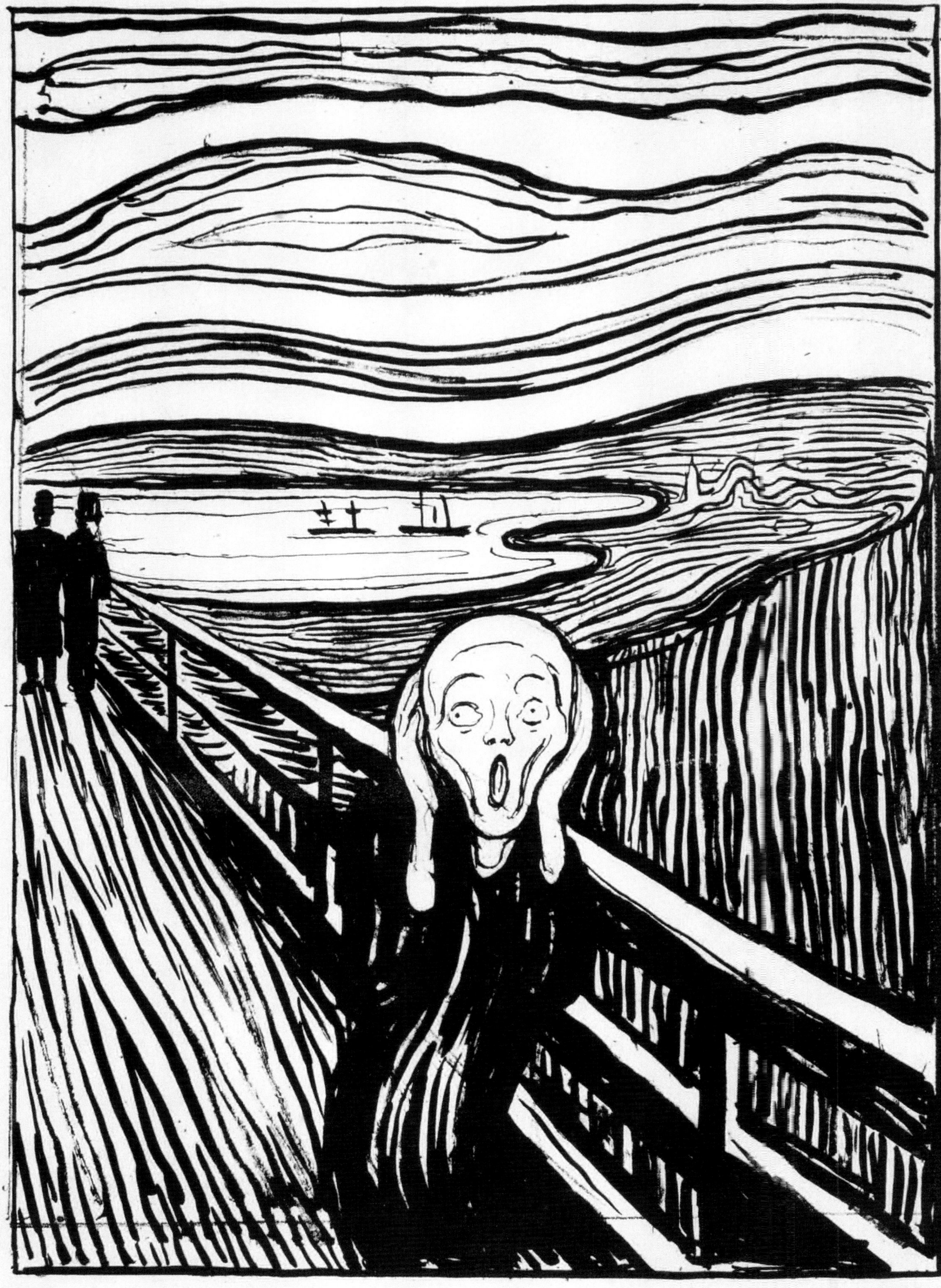

10 *Madonna*, 1895/1902, lithograph

The painting *Madonna* was central to the love section of Munch's 1895 Berlin exhibition. The lithograph was initially printed in black, but from 1902 Munch introduced colour from new stones. The woman confronts us frontally, rather like Psyche in Max Klinger's cycle *Cupid and Psyche* (1880). Madonna is depicted in the act of making love, and for many years the print was thought obscene. For Munch, the moment of conception was 'holy', and he wrote: 'Thus now life reaches out its hand to death. The chain is forged that binds the thousands of generations that have died to the thousands of generations yet to come' (T.2547).

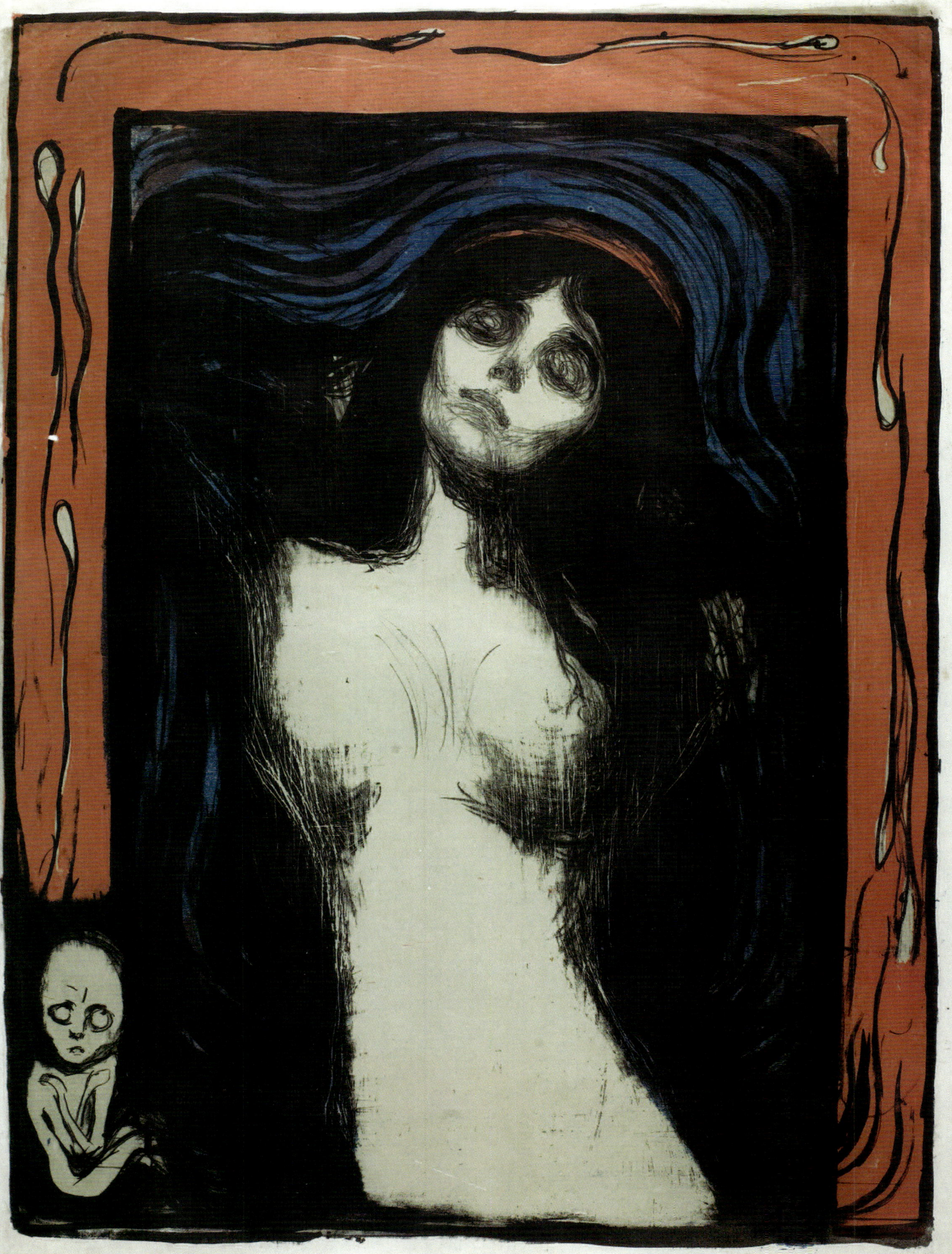

11 *Vampire II*, 1895, lithograph

First known as *Pain and Love, Vampire II* concerns the struggle between new lovers. Munch wrote of this: 'The woman's hair has wrapped itself around him and infiltrated his heart. The man is distraught by the struggle' (N 30). Przybyszewski gave the work its familiar literary title, and Strindberg, another friend and associate of Munch, in *La Revue Blanche* (June 1896) referred to Baudelaire's *Vampire*: 'Red Hair (Vampire): golden rain falls on the unfortunate kneeling creature who craves of his evil genius the boon of death by the prick of a needle. Golden fibres which bind to earth and to suffering. A rain of blood flows in torrents over the accursed head' (Hodin, 1972, 76).

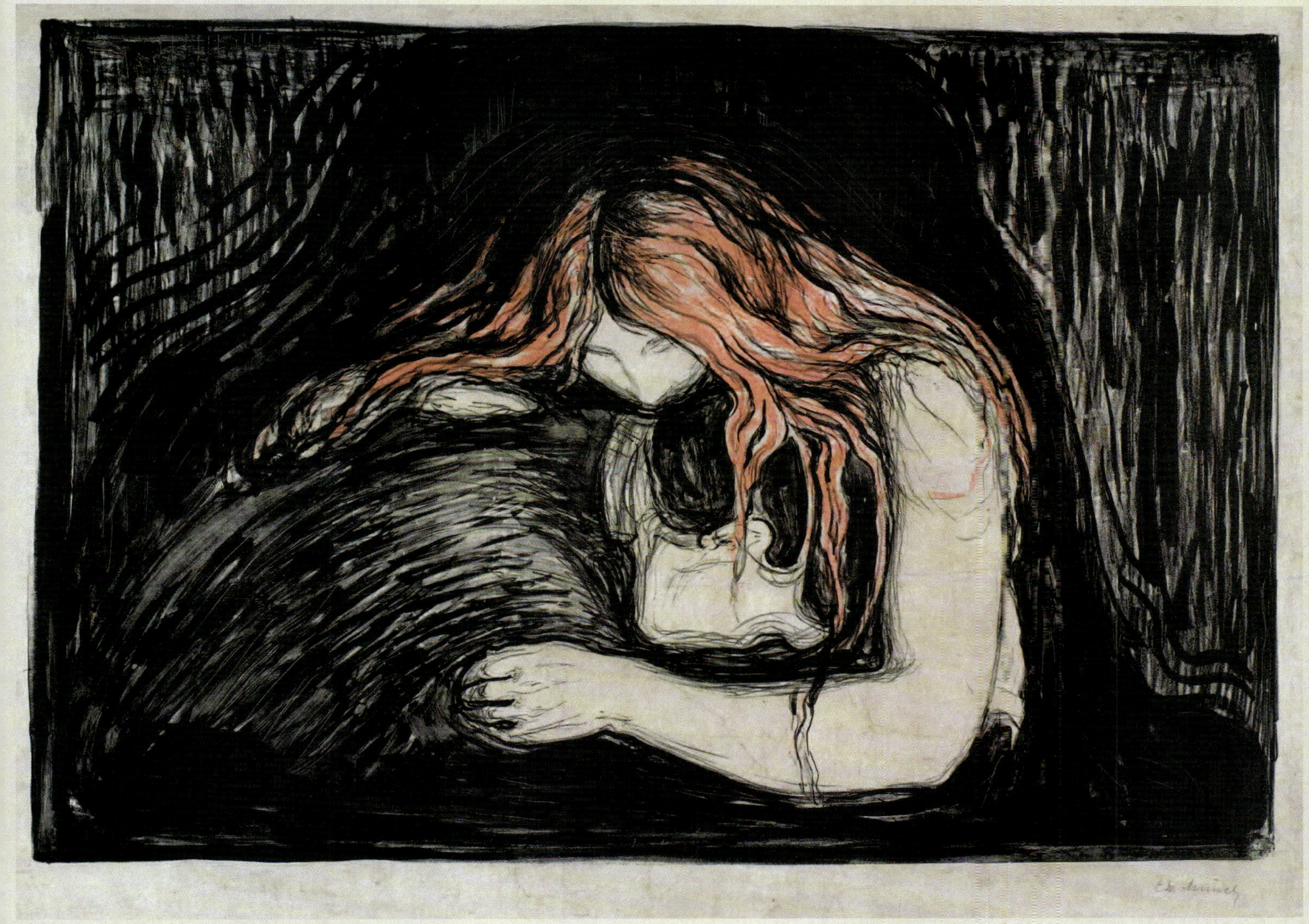

Bodenhausen (1868–1918) was strongly in favour of a German revival of printmaking. The graphic medium, he maintained, was superior in expressing the artist's innermost feelings. Another *Pan* member, Julius Meier-Graefe, was equally enthusiastic about the artistic possibilities of this medium, an enthusiasm that certainly must have had its impact on Munch.

In 1894, Munch was an established artist, though notorious rather than famous. His paintings were highly controversial, he sold very few of them and he was constantly short of money. However, nothing indicates that any expectations he may have had of making money quickly through printmaking were realised. Low sales and the use of skilled and expensive printers meant that profits were at best marginal during the first six or seven years. Regardless of this, he engaged himself vigorously in this field: with great artistic appetite he explored the different techniques, perfecting his skills in an astonishingly short time, and experimenting in a way that few of his contemporaries did.

The commercial aspect of Munch's graphic endeavour, therefore, should not be overplayed. A more important motivation would seem to be his genuine desire for people to know and understand his art better. Prints were cheaper and could be produced in much larger numbers than paintings. Most importantly, however, with printing he had found a medium that fascinated him and could convey his artistic message in a way that was different from and more condensed than his paintings.

12 *Stanislaw Przybyszewski*, 1895, lithograph
The Polish writer and medical student Stanislaw Przybyszewski (1868–1927) was a member of the avant-garde circle joined by Munch in Berlin in 1892. He published and contributed to the first book on Munch, with essays also written by Franz Servaes, Willy Pastor and Julius Meier-Graefe (1894). Przybyszewski had ideas about the transmission of thoughts as vibrations, which are given life by Munch in the waving lines of *The Scream*. Przybyszewski married Munch's friend the Norwegian musician Dagny Juel, with whom several of the Zum Schwarzen Ferkel group were in love. Przybyszewski's distinctive head was used by Munch in paintings on the theme of jealousy (15).

Intaglio

Munch's first prints were intaglio prints made with the simplest technique of all: drypoint. So simple is this method that he could even carry the needle and copperplate in his pocket, using it like a sketchbook. One of his very first prints, *Portrait of a Young Woman* (W. 2), may well have been executed in a café. In this exhibition, *Death and the Woman* (1) is an example of the pure drypoint technique. Very soon after this, however, he starts to expand his repertoire, first with tools such as the roulette and the burnisher, making possible tonal gradations not easily achieved in drypoint, then by turning to the more complicated method of etching – line etching as well as open bite – often in combination with drypoint. The need to prepare the plate with a wax ground, and afterwards mix an acid bath of exact strength and calculate

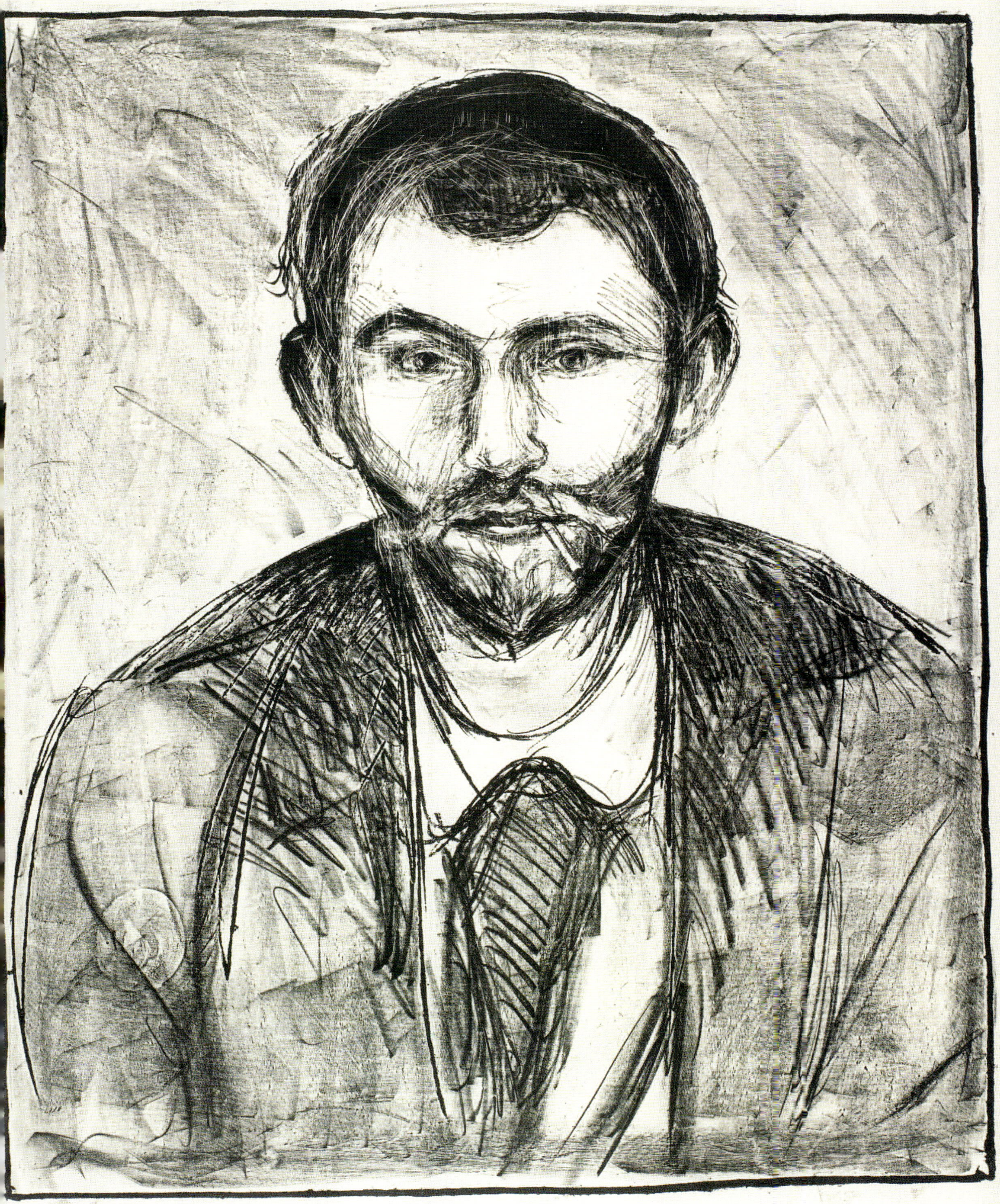

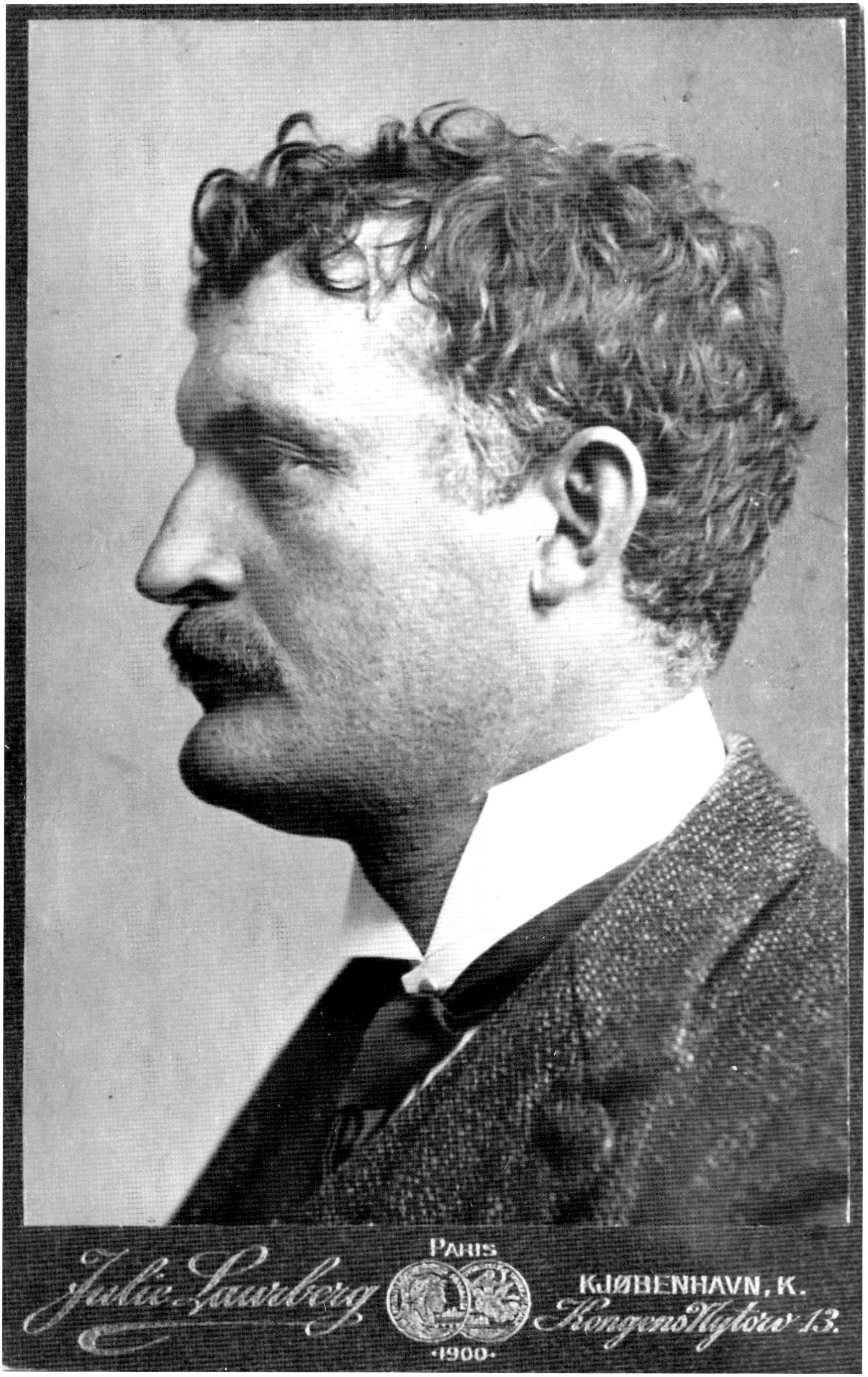
Julie Laurberg
PARIS
KJØBENHAVN, K.
Kongens Nytorv 13.
·1900·

the amount of time the plate spends in the bath makes this a more cumbersome method. On the other hand, the drawing on the plate can be executed with greater ease and fluency, and the effect of open bite, often in several steps, giving large areas different gradations of grey, seems to have appealed to Munch. This technique was used in many of his important intaglio prints, such as *The Day After* (2), *Summer Night. The Voice* (4), *Kristiania Bohemians II* (5), *Moonlight. Night in St Cloud* (6) and *Woman II* (7).

Julius Meier-Graefe – who was to become Germany's most celebrated art historian – is known to have been one of those who persuaded Munch to take up printmaking. In 1895 he went a stage further and published a portfolio containing eight of Munch's early intaglio prints, accompanied by a lengthy text on Munch as a printmaker. On the essence of prints, in contrast to paintings, he wrote: 'Like all decent engravings, these prints appear colourful, without any colour. One must be blind – or highly cultured – if one cannot recognise this effect in *The Lonely Ones, Tête-à-tête* or *Dawn* [*The Day After*] – all of them with the same subject as exceptionally good paintings, which one does not miss here.'[1]

Meier-Graefe here touches upon another aspect of Munch's graphic oeuvre: many of his prints – especially from his first years – are graphic versions of motifs already treated in paintings. This fact, however, does not make them less interesting as works of art. They are not printed reproductions, but motifs carefully translated and adapted to the specific qualities of another medium. Thus, just as his great project during the 1890s – later known as the *Frieze of Life* – may be exhibited in his paintings, it may also be exhibited in his graphic versions. The plural 'versions' is deliberate here; one of the effects of Munch's almost childlike joy in experimenting was that impressions of the same print might be very different. This becomes particularly evident in his colour woodcuts, but even with the intaglio prints there are variations in paper quality, paper colour and inking. Some impressions are hand coloured, whilst others are not, and the majority of his intaglio prints are found in a number of different states, i.e. impressions pulled at various stages of the artist's work on the plate.

One of Munch's most evocative intaglio prints – and one that is faintly reminiscent of some of Whistler's night visions – is *Moonlight.*

1 Gerd Woll, *Edvard Munch, 1895, First Year as a Graphic Artist* (Oslo: Munch Museum, 1995), 33–4.

Fig. 3 Portrait of Munch in profile, c.1910

Night in St Cloud (6). This image is normally associated with his sorrow on receiving the news of his father's death, but may just as well be regarded as a general embodiment of melancholy and sadness, which exploits the contrast between the gloomy room and the moonlit world outside. Meier-Graefe expresses this point well when he writes: 'A man is sitting at the window, grey in grey, a small piece of twilight, completely absorbed by the shadow, by the melancholy obtaining in the room, a quivering breath. He sits and thinks. And the physical part of him disappears, he becomes one with his thoughts, and with the soft, inner glances. He might well dissolve; he is looking at the moon, and the moon has infected him.'[2]

Lithography

Only a few weeks after making his first drypoints, Munch took up lithography. Two obvious advantages of this technique might have attracted him: first, drawing with lithographic crayon on stone is just as easy as with pencil on paper and, second, one can pull a much larger number of impressions than is possible with intaglio prints in general, and drypoints in particular. In addition to these technical advantages, lithography produces something that comes much closer to looking like a drawing than intaglio prints, and drawing was an integral part of Munch's artistic identity – he exhibited drawings and made them in large numbers, almost anytime, anywhere. Here, therefore, he found a medium that could reliably translate drawings to prints.

Munch started to make lithographs while still in Berlin. Paris was, of course, the pivotal city for the new artistic interest in original lithography, but even in Berlin its waves were being felt. The Radiervereine (Graphic Associations) began to publish portfolios of lithographs, and influential painter-printmakers like Max Liebermann started to expand their graphic repertoires with lithographs.

As with Munch's early intaglio prints, versions based on major paintings constitute a large part of his lithographic production in the 1890s: *The Scream* (9), *Madonna* (10), *Vampire II* (11), *Angst*, *Death in the Sickroom* (13), *Jealousy I* (15) and *The Sick Child I* (16), to mention only a few. Of all Munch's graphic works,

13 *Death in the Sickroom*, 1896, lithograph

This work was made in Paris in the first group of lithographs made with Clot; the Munch Museum has a preparatory drawing of 1893/4 (T 2380). The sickroom image was developed from Munch's memories of the death of his elder sister Sophie who died in 1877, when he was fourteen. Munch (in profile) and his sisters appear older than they were. His father and aunt stand either side of the dying Sophie, who is seated to the right. The composition is a staging of a remembered event, reminiscent of Symbolist dramas by writers such as Maeterlinck, whose plays were in Munch's library.

2 Ibid., 38–39.

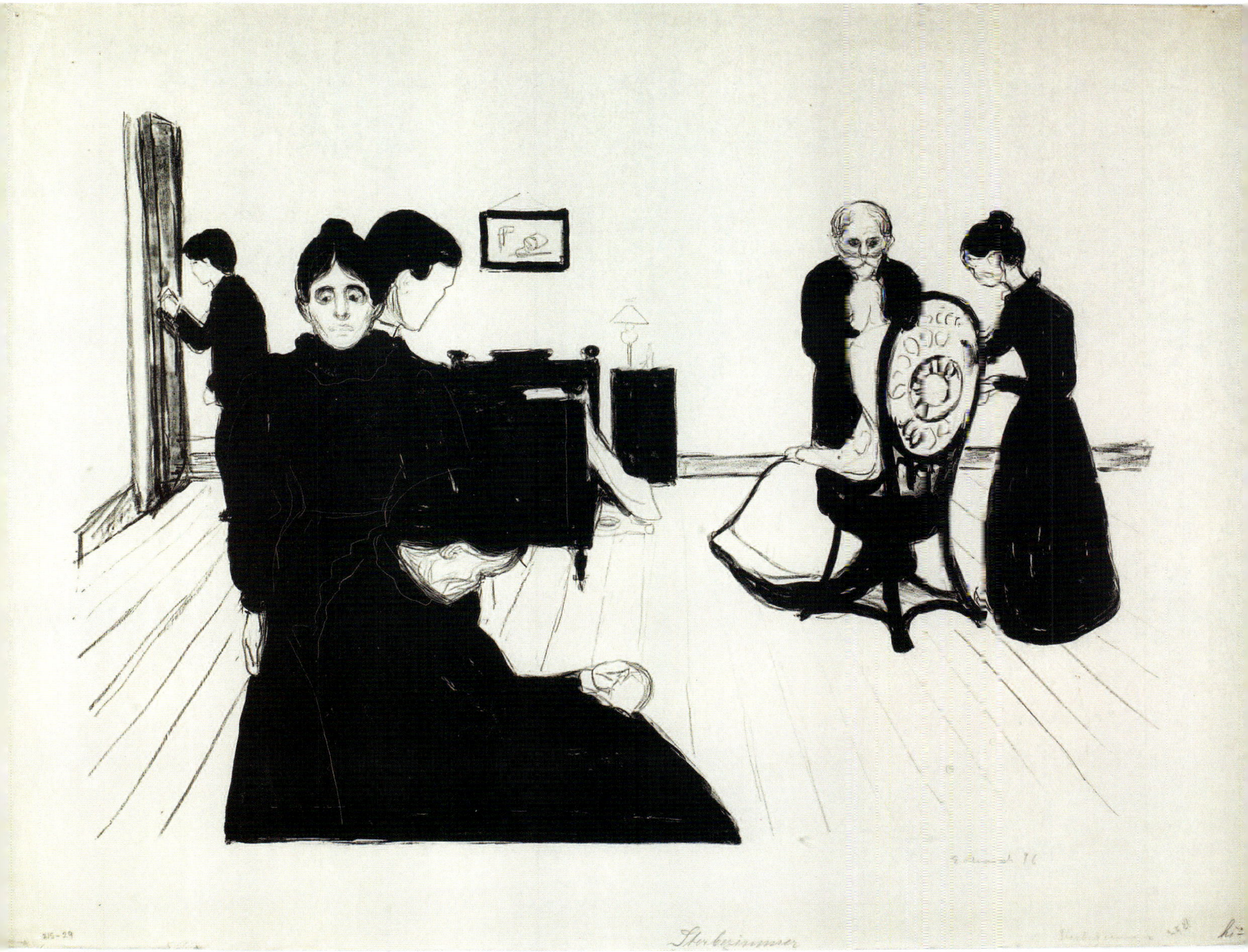
Sterbezimmer

Madonna was without a doubt the best-selling motif. We estimate that there are between 250 and 300 copies in existence today, over half of which were either sold or given away. He also made sure to keep a large and varied selection for himself, however, which accounts for why the Munch Museum has 115 impressions in its collection today. The great number of variations – in format, colour combination and state – demonstrates not only Munch's joy in experimentation, but also how much this motif meant to him. Nearly twenty years passed before he was appeased and concluded work on this print.

In the mid-1890s, Munch was, in Christian terms, an agnostic, but he was nevertheless occupied with spiritual subject matter: the big questions of life and death. The question 'What is sacred?' is central to him and his work, though his answer to it was highly controversial:

> I was to paint two persons in the most sacred moment of their lives – where they had been seized by the power that is stronger than anything else – that which has the colour of the rose but is stronger than death – In that moment we are not ourselves […] I wanted the audience to feel that this was a sacred moment – and to take their hats off as they do in a church.[3]

14 *August Strindberg*, 1896, lithograph

Strindberg (1849–1912), the Swedish playwright, arrived in Berlin, like Munch, in 1892. Strindberg encouraged Munch to make prints, having previously collaborated with the printmaker Karl Larsson. Munch has set Strindberg's powerful head within a fashionable Art-Nouveau border mirroring Strindberg's wiry hair. Out of the zigzag lines, Munch has symbolically conjured a naked woman, as if she is central to his thoughts. The masklike woodcut *In the Man's Brain* (24) again shows the male obsession with the female body. The irascible Strindberg was annoyed by Munch's misspelling of his name and by the border. Both were later corrected.

Despite his good intentions, however, *Madonna* was widely considered blasphemous. The title connected the Virgin Mary with the sex act, and the depiction of sperm and embryos on the painting's frame was definitely taboo. The frame with these ornaments, which probably decorated the first painted version, was subsequently removed, and the titles *Loving Woman* and *Monna* (!) were also used in an attempt to comply with public opinion. However, the authentic title is important because it sends a clear message: the moment when new life is created is sacred, and the woman becomes sacred because this takes place inside her body. Munch wrote several textual versions for most of his central paintings, and for *Madonna* he wrote:

> Your face contains all the tenderness of the world – The Moonlight shines softly on your face that is full of earthly Beauty and Pain. Because now Death gives a Hand to Life

3 Note in the Munch Museum, MM N 289.

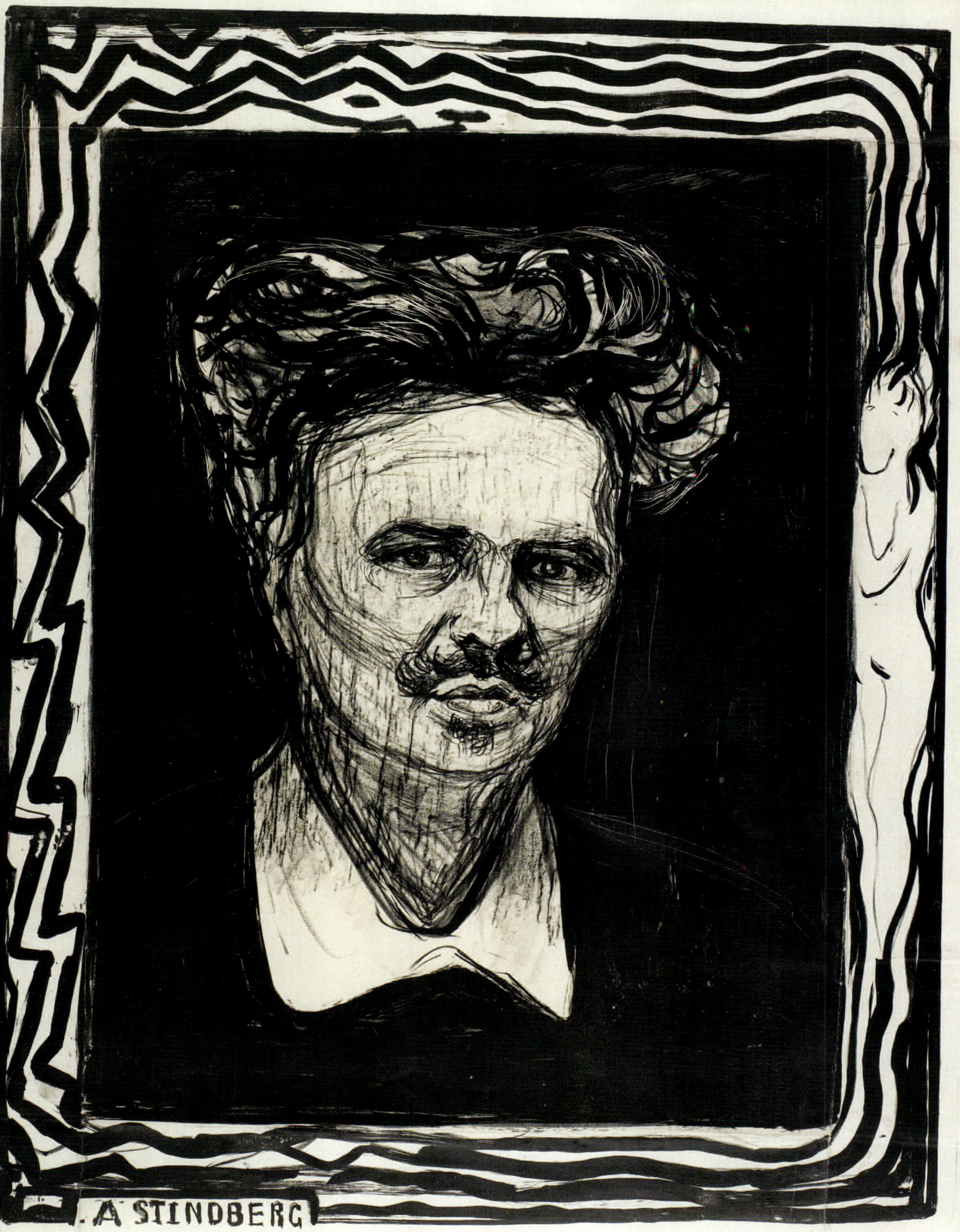
A STINDBERG

Fig. 4 Lithographic stone for jealousy I (15)

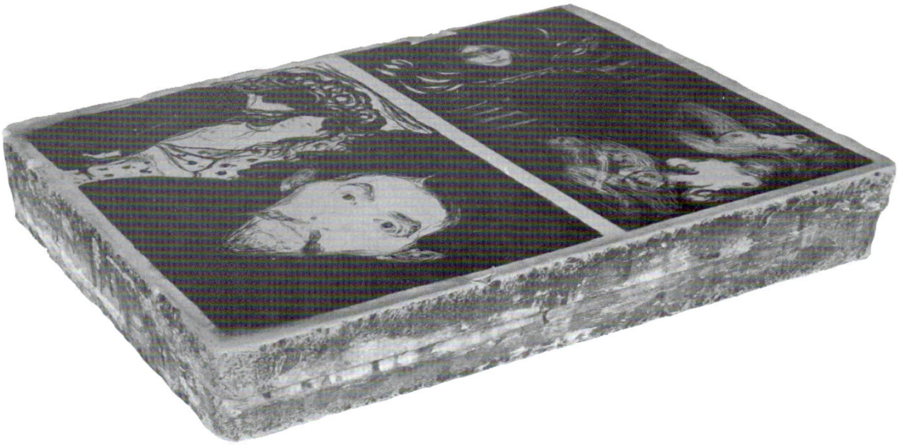

and a bond is knit between the thousands of Generations that are gone and the thousands of Generations to come.[4]

If this is the moment of conception, we would expect the presence of a man as well. And why is she standing? The point is, she is not. She is lying down and a man is bending over her: she is seen through his eyes. This is Munch's version of the first person narrative technique so frequently used in the literature of this period. It is subjective and renders space and identity in a way that is different from the traditional third person perspective. Yet *On the Waves of Love* (19) and *The Kiss IV* (33), both of which belong to this series of motifs, have the same intensity as *Madonna*, though, technically speaking, the perspective of both is more 'objective'.

The Scream is among the most thoroughly analysed and interpreted paintings in the history of art. It is also among the most frequently exhibited as an original, a reproduction and a caricature, in a number of variations. We have seen it so often that really *seeing* it has become difficult; we have grown almost immune to its powerful impact. Perhaps, then, it is a good idea to fix our eyes – in as far as it is possible with this work of art – on an original version that is different from the strongly-coloured painted versions. For once, let us not burden the onlooker with comments other than Munch's own:

I was out walking with two friends – then the sun settled – the sky suddenly turned blood red – I stopped, leaning on the fence dead-tired – There were blood and fire tongues

15 *Jealousy I*, 1896, lithograph
Jealousy is a central strand of Munch's love theme. Munch's pictures relate closely to the psychological dramas of his playwright friend August Strindberg. *Jealousy I* depicts a love triangle that partly reflects Munch's own experience. Munch's friend Przybyszewski, whose head stares out at us, adhered to Bohemian ideas about free love, tolerating the affairs of his partner Dagny Juel. In the background we witness an entanglement between Przybyszewski's partner Dagny and her lover (who has Munch's features). This is presented as a scene imagined inside Przybyszewski's head, a device also used in *Melancholy III* (32).

4 Note in the Munch Museum, MM T 2782 ar.

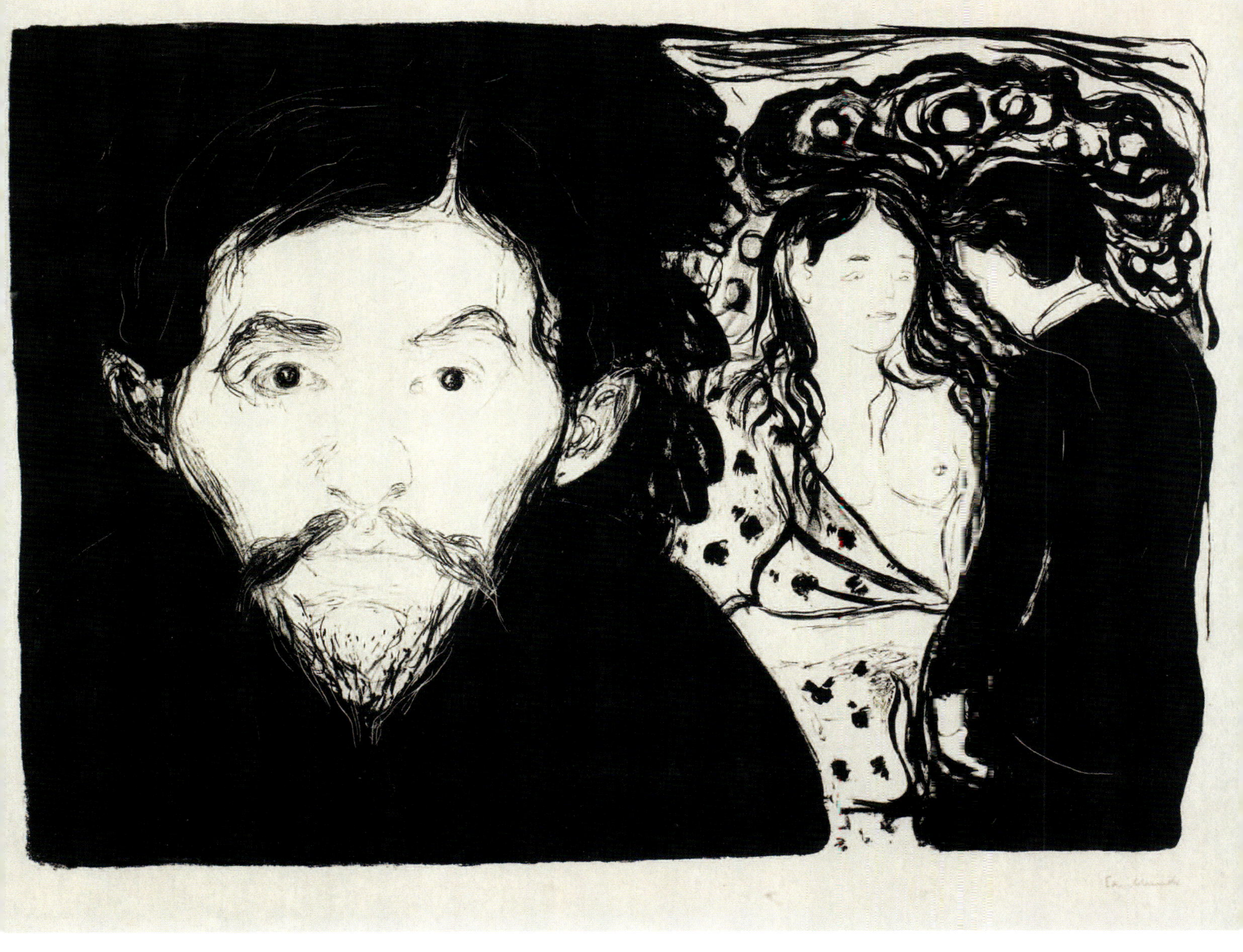

above the bluish black fjord – my friends walked on and again I was trembling with anxiety – I sensed a loud endless scream through nature.[5]

Portraits

The very first painting Munch exhibited publicly was a portrait, *Study of a Head* (1883). She was not exactly a feminine beauty, and critics disliked the painting, but the critic who wrote in the *Dagbladet* (*The Daily Mail*), noticed Munch's ability to portray the inner personality of the sitter. According to him, the girl in the painting was 'red-haired, small-eyed, ugly, but full of character, very lifelike.' This first critical review of a work by Munch contained one typical aspect: even critics who felt nothing but aversion for his art in general had to recognise the expressive power and keen characterisation of his portraits. Gradually he became one of the most sought-after portraitists at home as well as on the continent.

His portraits display his own genuine perception of the sitter's character, often – but not always – combined with a striking physical resemblance. Indeed, he could be quite merciless towards the person he portrayed, especially if this person happened to be himself. In her catalogue essay for the 2005 exhibition of self-portraits, Munch by Himself, Iris Müller-Westermann ranks Munch among the great self-portrait artists, 'the doubters, interrogators and prophets from Rembrandt through Goya to Van Gogh.' Moreover, she continues, '… Munch's self-portraits occupy a special place in art history. He was the first painter to use his art to analyse his emotional state comprehensively; exploring all its depths and manifold nuances.'[6] The two self-portraits in this selection, the lithographs *Self-portrait* (8) from 1895 and *Self-portrait with a Bottle of Wine* (41) from 1930 stand as good representatives of this part of his oeuvre. The former depicts a self-confident and self-assured young artist, very much alive, but with the presence of death even here. The name and year above the hovering head highlight the concepts of life and time, while the skeletal arm below represents those of death and eternity. The later *Self-portrait with a*

16 *The Sick Child I*, 1896, lithograph

In 1896 Munch moved to Paris to make lithographs. Among the first masterpieces is this final statement of the *Sick Child* subject, which was first painted in 1885-6 as a memorial to his sister Sophie (13). It is exceptional, being Munch's only true colour lithograph. *The Sick Child I* was printed by Auguste Clot, who had that year printed Munch's lithograph *Angst* (W. 63) for Vollard's print portfolio. It treats the subject in the same direction as the painting, and on a grander scale than the drypoint (W. 7). The focus on the girl's head is more intense, her features made up of wraithlike crayon-lines, fading into the pillow on which she rests.

5 Note in the Munch Museum, MM T 2367.

6 Iris Müller-Westermann, *Munch by Himself* (London: Royal Academy Books, 2005), 15–16.

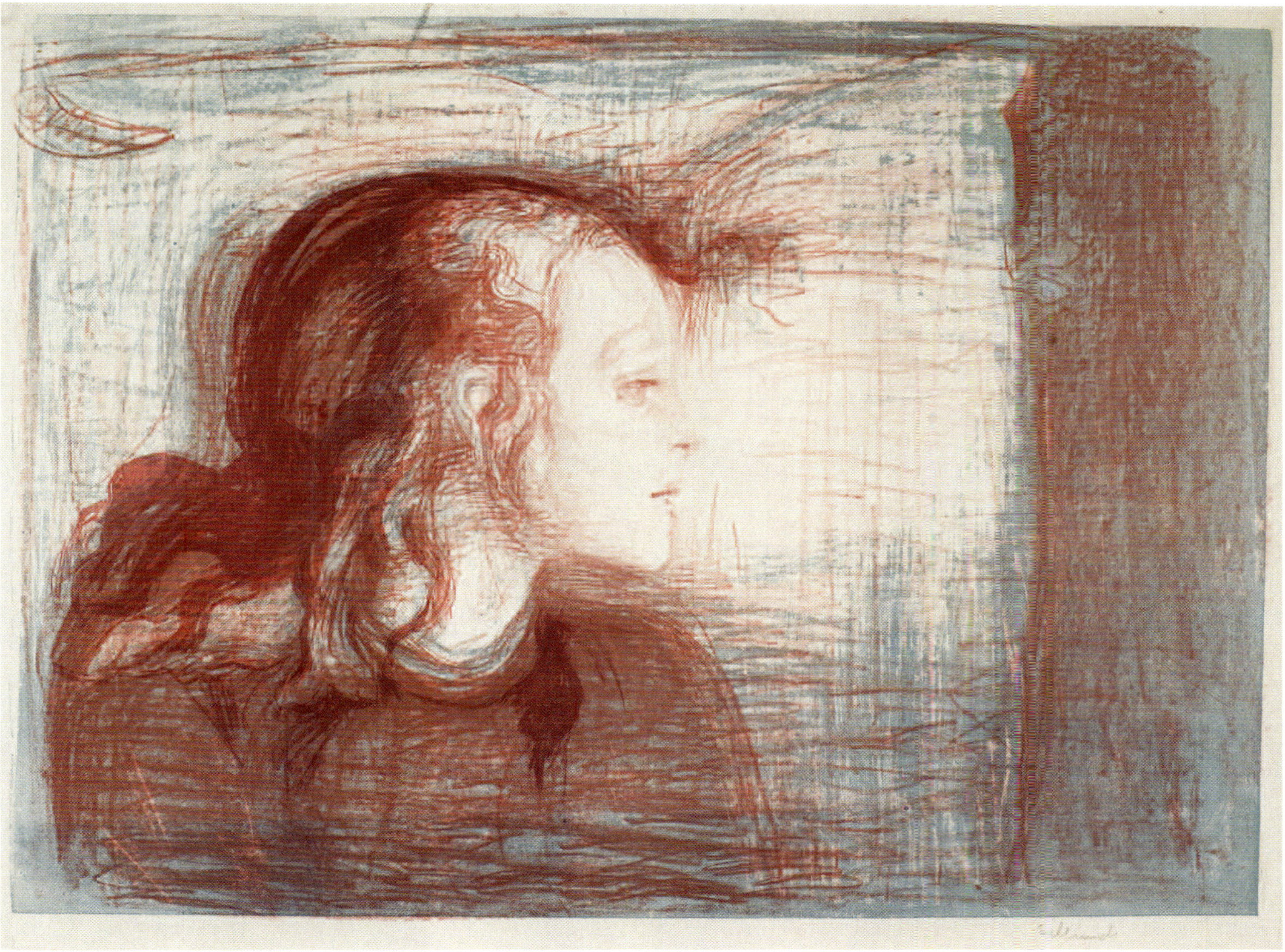

Bottle of Wine, underscores the feelings of loneliness and inner tension. It is, by contrast, an image of weakness, his passive hands being artistically just as dead as the skeletal arm in the earlier self-portrait.

All of the portraits shown here are lithographs. Whilst Munch did make a number of intaglio portraits, and some expressive ones in woodcut, lithography seems to have suited him particularly well for his portraits. The impulsiveness of the drawing technique might be one reason for this, but lithography offers one possibility that is absent in intaglio and woodcut, and which is of importance with regard to portraits: the image can be drawn initially on a piece of paper, before being transferred to the stone and subsequently printed. In this manner the image is reversed twice, ending up the same way round as it was drawn. We often think of a face as being regular and symmetrical, but in fact there are any number of small irregularities: one eye may be slightly different from the other, a wrinkle on the left side may curl differently from the one on the right, and the parting of the hair or even the basic shape of the skull may be asymmetrical. Such easily unnoticed irregularities can be difficult to represent 'mirrored', as one has to in intaglio prints and woodcuts, but when drawing on transfer paper this is no longer a problem: the face, with all of its imperfections, will be rendered exactly as drawn. Whether this was an important consideration for Munch or not is difficult to say, but the fact remains that a large majority of his lithographic portraits are transfer lithographs of this kind. In this exhibition this is true of *Stéphane Mallarmé* (23), *Ibsen at the Grand Café* (31) and *Friedrich Nietzsche* (36). *Stanislaw Przybyszewski* (12) and *August Strindberg* (14), on the other hand, are not of this type, though this can be explained by the fact that Munch may have executed them before he became acquainted with the transfer technique.

The prospect of cooperating with the best lithographic printers, as well as being a part of the most advanced graphic milieu, may well have been one of the motivations for Munch's transfer from Berlin to Paris in February 1896. Without hesitation, he engaged the master printer Auguste Clot for the printing of his newly made lithographs – *Angst, By the Deathbed, Death in the Sickroom, August Strindberg, Jealousy I* and *Jealousy II.* Besides receiving first-class impressions of these central works, Munch would also have gained the best information available about the technical procedures of lithography.

17 *Attraction I,* 1896, lithograph

Man and woman are reduced to a pair of symbols, as large-eyed heads on the shore at Åsgårdstrand, the village which often forms the backdrop for Munch's emotional dramas. White strands of the woman's hair, engraved into the surface of the lithographic stone, entwine the man and bind him to her. Two stars are prominent in the night sky. A note by Munch compares the joining of lovers with stars: 'A pair of stars that is fated to meet strays towards one another only for a moment, then each disappears to its ownregion in the vastness of space' (N 30, 1894–6).

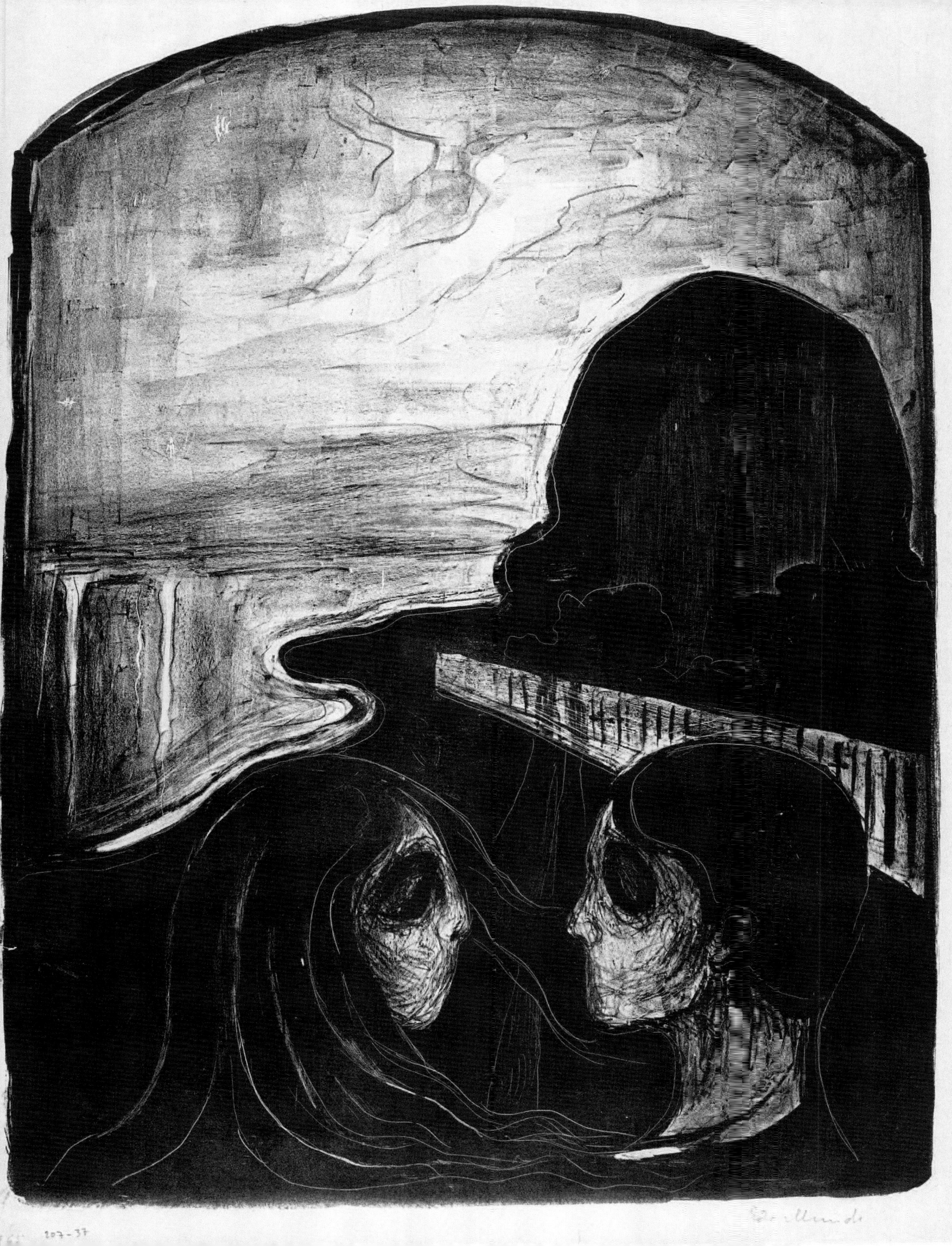
207-37

18 *Separation II*, 1896, lithograph

Munch's love scenes are frequently set on the seashore, with his lovers' heads close together. Here the relationship has cooled, and the motif of strands of hair binding man and woman now stands– for a permanent emotional tie that will bind the couple even when separated. Munch wrote of this and related images:

Jealousy, an immense desolate beach.
The woman's hair has wrapped itself around
Him and infiltrated his heart.
The man is distraught by the struggle (N 30).

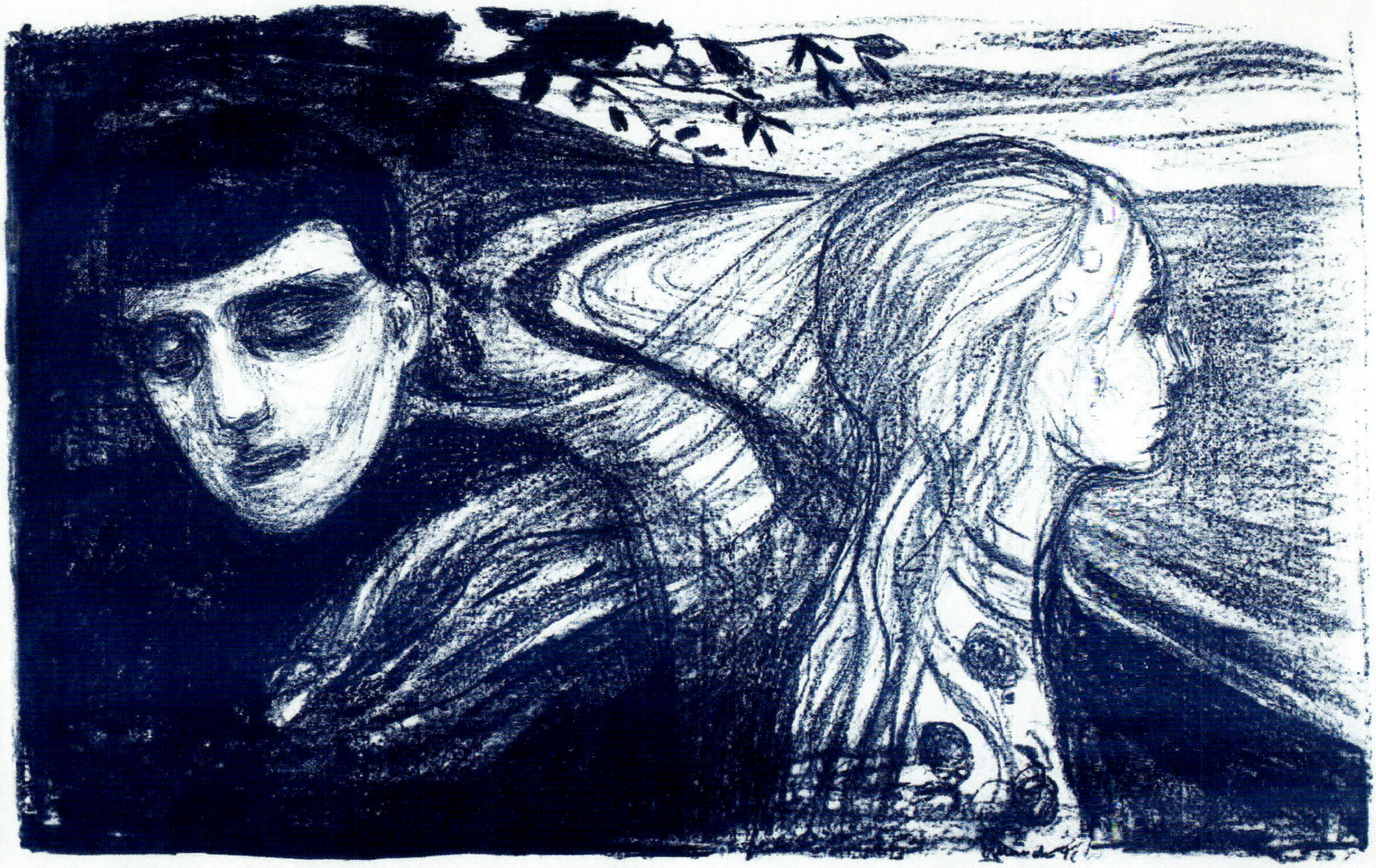

19 *On the Waves of Love*, 1896, lithograph

The waves are Munch's response to the idea of his friend Stanislaw Przybyszewski (12) that thoughts are transmitted as vibrations. Munch used waving lines in several pictures of the 1890s, including *The Scream* (9) and *Madonna* (10). The act of love depicted in this print and in the closely related early version of *Madonna* (3) is something that Munch likened to waves in one of his poetic writings:

Like one – body we glide out upon
a vast ocean – on long waves which
change in colour
from deep violet to blood red
(T. 2547–64).

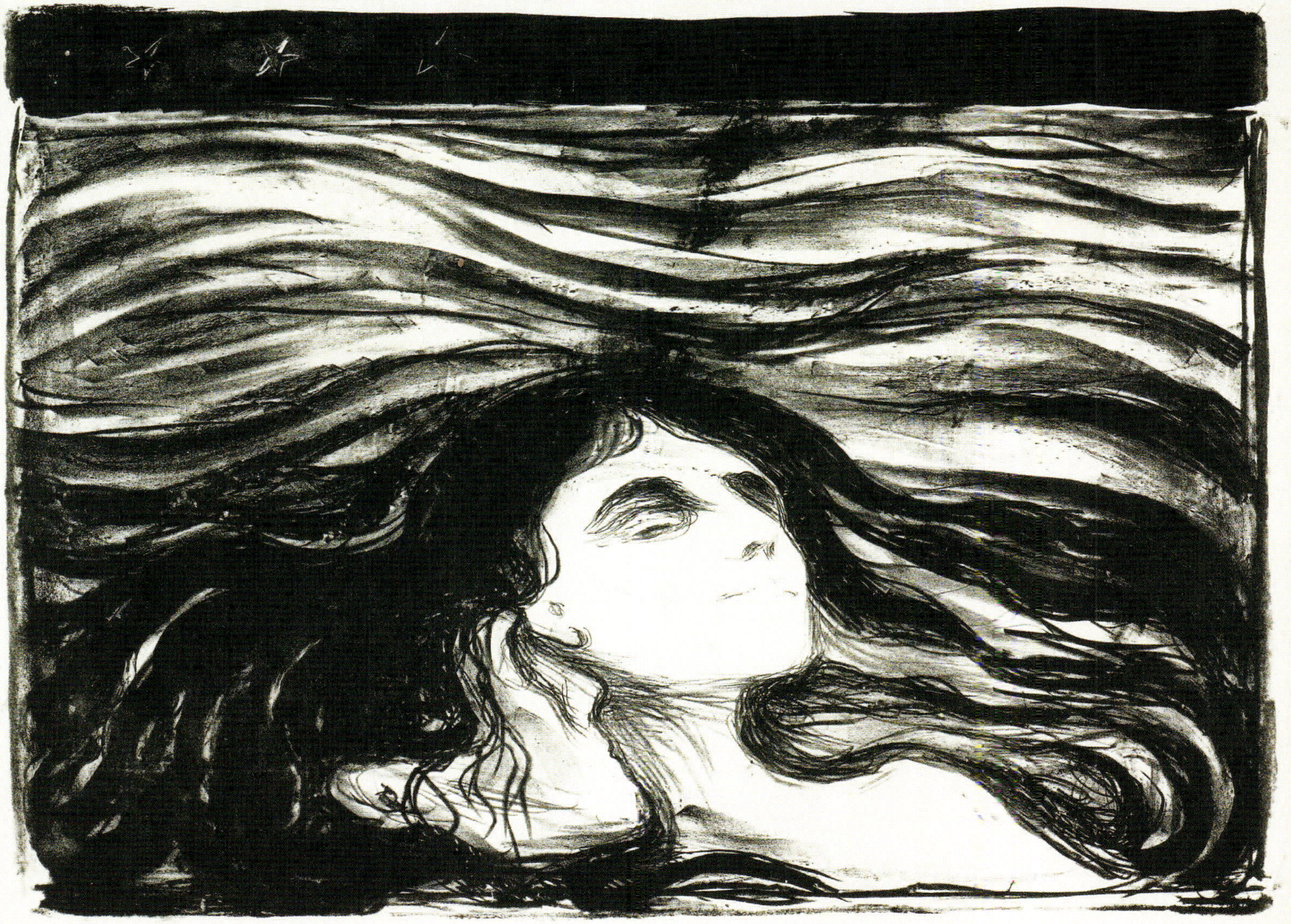

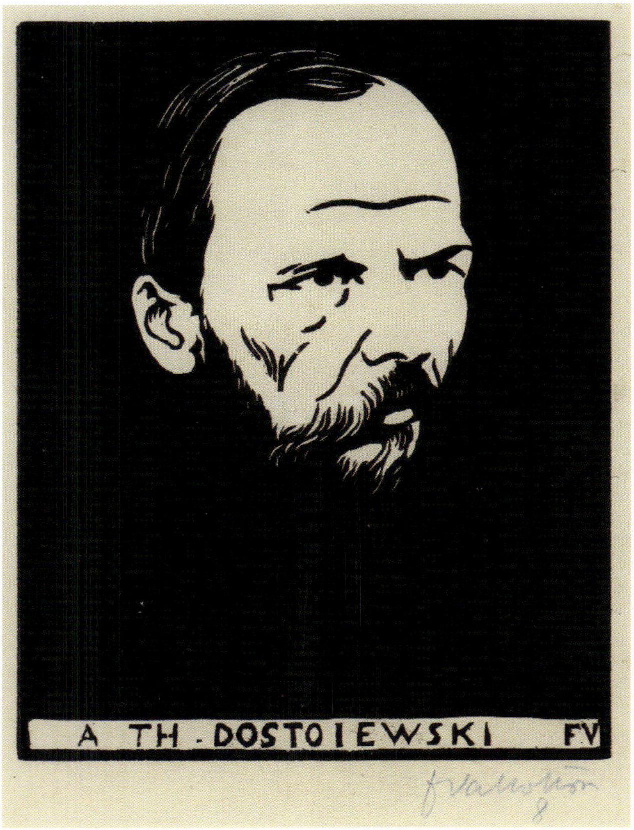

Fig. 5 Félix Vallotton, *A Th. Dostoiewski*, 1895, wood engraving, Cabinet d'Estampes, Musées d'Art et d'Histoire, Geneva

Before long he was absorbed in work on his most ambitious colour lithograph, *The Sick Child*. With a single keystone as a basis, he made five different colour stones, enabling him to create an almost indefinite number of colour combinations. While the painting from 1885–86 shows an interior with two people, the lithograph concentrates on the sick girl's head. The sick and dying constituted a popular genre subject in international art, but Munch abandons all of the demonstrative gestures that are so common in these depictions. With delicate and sensitive lines he interprets the silent despair and wonder of a young girl who feels life fading away before she herself is allowed to blossom.

Woodcuts

The oldest printing technique – woodcut – was the last one that Munch took up. However, it immediately caught his imagination, and it was in this field that he was at his most innovative and where his influence on other graphic artists was greatest. It is also in his woodcuts that he truly liberates himself from the influence of his own paintings. He may still give graphic life to a number of his painted motifs, it is true, but the independence of these from their models and their distinctive graphic characters are now even greater. It is in his woodcuts that he consistently and consciously turns his back on naturalism, creating a pictorial language that is unusually direct, strong in its appeal, and possessed of a power of expression seldom found in the art of his contemporaries.

What, or who, we may ask, prompted him to turn to woodblocks and gouges? In 1896, woodcuts were not commonly made by artist printmakers, but they were slowly gaining ground. Japanese prints had been rousing the interest of collectors and artists, and had even influenced European oil painting. Gauguin had chosen woodcut and wood engraving as his preferred mode of graphic expression, and the Swiss artist Félix Vallotton (1865–1925) built his artistic reputation more on his characteristic woodcut style than on his paintings. In fact, it seems obvious that Vallotton had exercised a profound influence on Munch even before the latter started making woodcuts. While most graphic artists tried to give a large tonal range to their prints, Vallotton radically reduced his woodcuts to simplified forms of black and white. The same approach is characteristic of a number of Munch's lithographs, such as *The Scream*, *Angst*, *Jealousy I*, *By the Deathbed*, *Death in the Sickroom* and *Self-portrait*. It is tempting to believe that Munch saw Vallotton's portrait *A. Th. Dostoiewski* (fig. 5) before he made his lithographic self-portrait, but both were created in 1895, so it is more reasonable to believe that here we have an example of two artists tuned to the same artistic wavelength, even if they were working in different media.

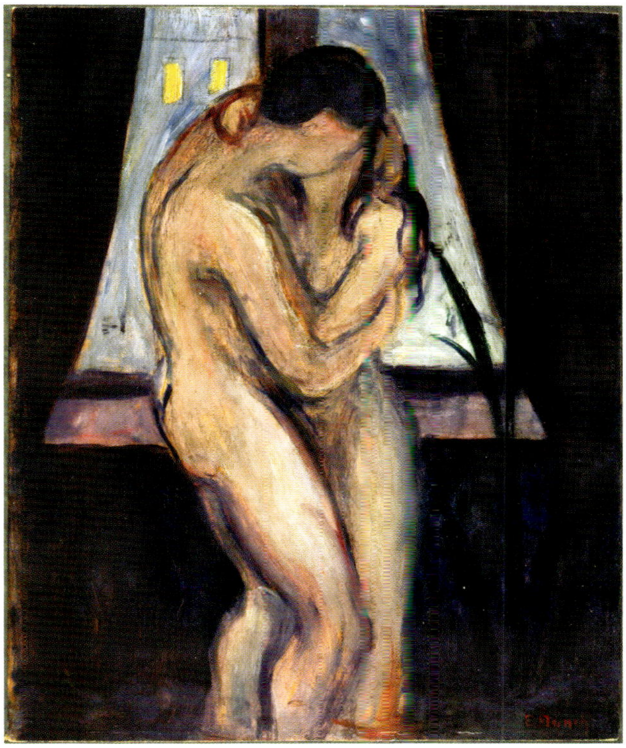

Fig. 6 *The Kiss*, 1896–97, oil on canvas, Munch Museum, PEO 263

People are so accustomed to the fine tonal gradations in lithographs that some works, notably *The Scream* and the lithographic version of *Angst*, have occasionally been misinterpreted as woodcuts. This misinterpretation, though false, points up an important truth about Munch's transition from lithograph to woodcut: this is the medium in which he could refine and cultivate the simplicity for which he had always searched. One feels that in woodcut some of his central motifs found their purest and finest formulation. Complex symbols and strong emotions are condensed into strikingly simple figurative formulas. The painted version of *The Kiss* (fig. 6) is strong and beautiful, yet it is so lifelike that one expects the couple to end their embrace at any moment. In the woodcut version, on the other hand, they have become 'one flesh', locked together for eternity. Even in its extreme simplicity, the motif has not been reduced to something superficial, but transformed into an iconic symbol of love.

This print also demonstrates a quality typical of Munch's woodcuts: the structure of the wood is allowed to play an active part in the pictorial expression. Thus, far from trying to hide the characteristics of the material, he invites nature to play along, underscoring the natural qualities of the medium. The choice of wood is also important for this: soft woods, such as spruce and pine, are well suited, and by polishing the surface gently with sandpaper and using thin, water-based ink, it is possible to get the wood grain to stand out, as it does so conspicuously in this impression of *The Kiss IV*.

Munch's restless and impatient artistic temperament made him look for shortcuts and ways of simplifying traditional techniques. Thus, instead of making a new woodblock for each colour, he divided the block into several pieces using a fretsaw, inked them separately, 'puzzled' them together again, and in this way produced multicoloured prints from one block. This simplified the process, but more importantly, it simplified the visual expression of the work, gathering the pictorial elements in a few, pregnant forms. This is beautifully exemplified in *Two Human Beings. The Lonely Ones* (29), but even *Moonlight I* (20), *Evening. Melancholy I* (21), *Melancholy III* (32), *Two Women on the Shore* (26), *Woman's Head against the Shore* (28) and *Moonlight by the Sea* (38) are 'puzzle woodcuts'.

Some describe paintings as prose and graphic works as poems, and the comparison is not without validity: formally simpler, more concentrated and with an added attention to rhythm, prints often have a distinctive lyrical quality. This is not to say that Munch's canvases lack such a quality, but many feel that it can be best enjoyed in his graphic works. This variation of Munch's 'voice' that we detect in different versions of his images, in oil on canvas or prints from copper, stone or wood, is of the utmost importance. Munch embarked on making prints in 1894 after he had, in many cases, already executed the images as paintings. Prints became one more way in which he recast his images. The process began in Berlin, where Munch's first prints emerged alongside the written and printed contributions of his friends August Strindberg, Richard Dehmel, Julius Meier-Graefe and Stanislaw Przybyszewski, and resorting to print must have seemed a promising route to fame and success. Throughout his long career, Munch remained wedded to this process of reliving, rethinking and re-presenting his imagery, painted and printed. Indeed, it is one of his defining characteristics.

20 *Moonlight I*, 1896, woodcut
Munch's first woodcuts (21, 22) were made in Paris in 1896. A woman's face shines in a shaft of moonlight, with beautiful dark colouring reminiscent of nocturnal landscapes by the Swiss painter Arnold Böcklin (1827–1901). The woman has the features of Munch's first love, Milly Thaulow, a married woman with whom he had a love affair in 1885. The artist refers to her in his notes as Mrs Heiberg, and the memories haunted him for years. Milly is also the remembered subject of the early etching *Summer Night. The Voice* (4).

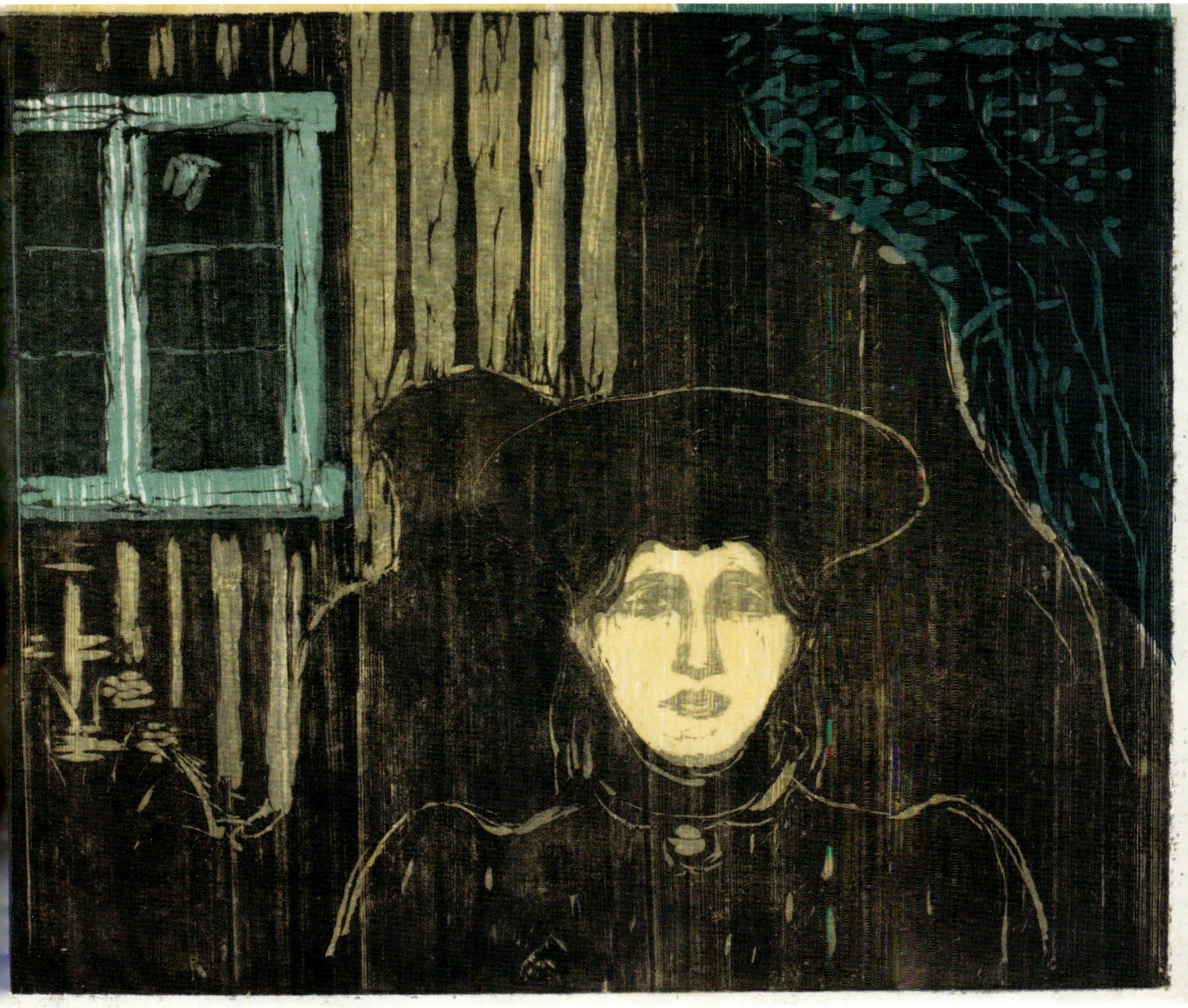

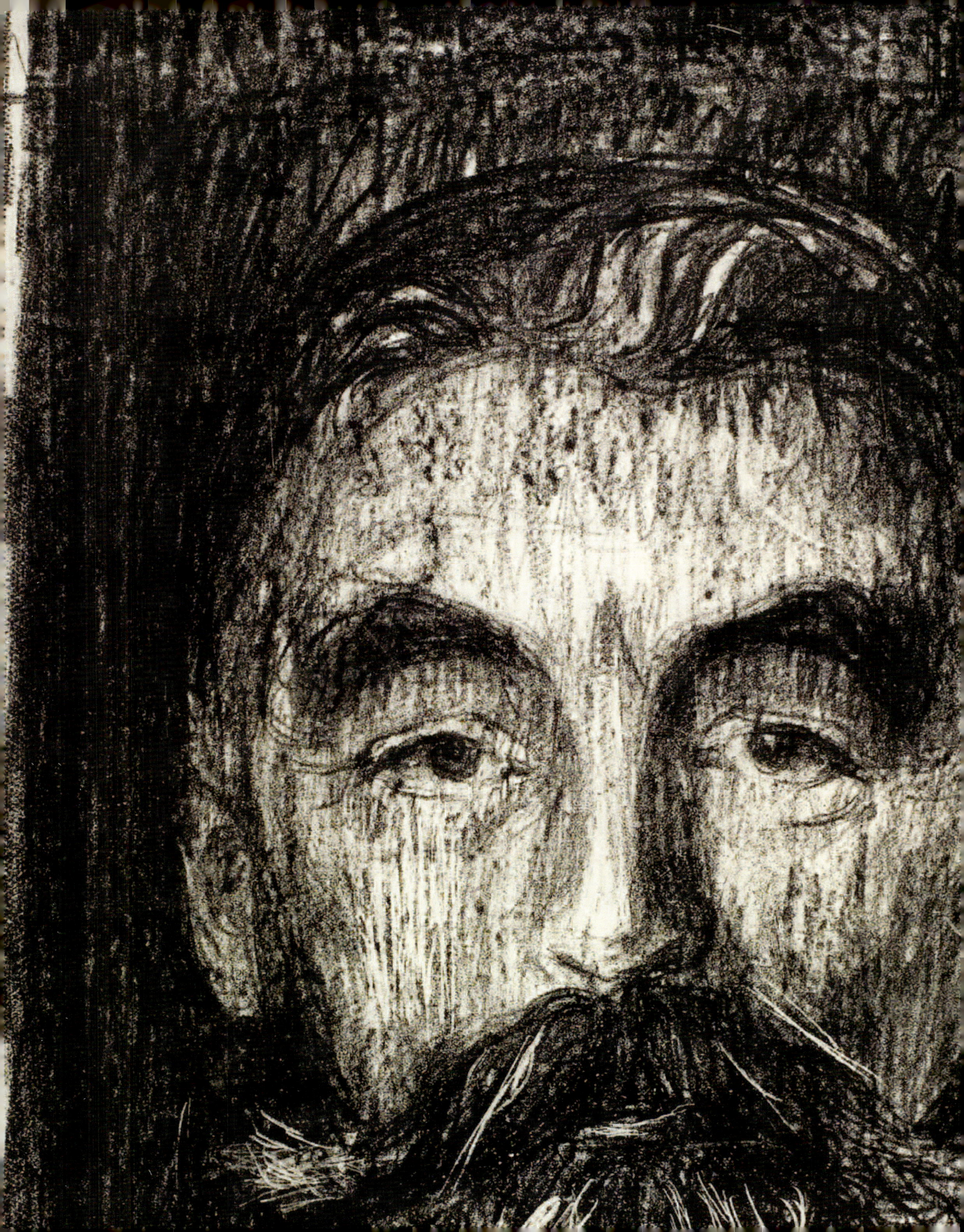

Munch's Woodcuts and Their Influence on German Printmaking

PETER BLACK

Munch began to make woodcuts a few years after his first etchings and lithographs. From now on, wood will long remain his preferred means of expression … In the woodcut, colour is now also established as an expressive symbol.

Curt Glaser, *Edvard Munch*

It was Munch whose woodcuts, with their rough and simple expressive qualities, inspired the great phase of printmaking that is such an important part of German Expressionist art. Quite exceptionally, in the period 1906–39, major German artists gave prints – frequently woodcuts – primary importance in their exhibitions. Munch did not start out making woodcuts, however, but his adoption of the new technique is hardly surprising given the precocity with which he took on virtually every print technique, producing a remarkable number of masterpieces in this medium in the years 1894–96. Munch was more determined to become known for his lithographs than for any other kind of print, but he began to make woodcuts in 1896–97 – which does not quite support the drastic change of direction that Glaser suggests in the epigraph at the head of the chapter – because of his discovery of a relatively simple technique that was ideally suited to his imagery, in which mood, and therefore colour, were essential. Woodcut offered the possibility of colour without the complexities of production associated with lithography – the heavy stones, the chemical etching, and

Stéphane Mallarmé (detail), 1897, lithograph

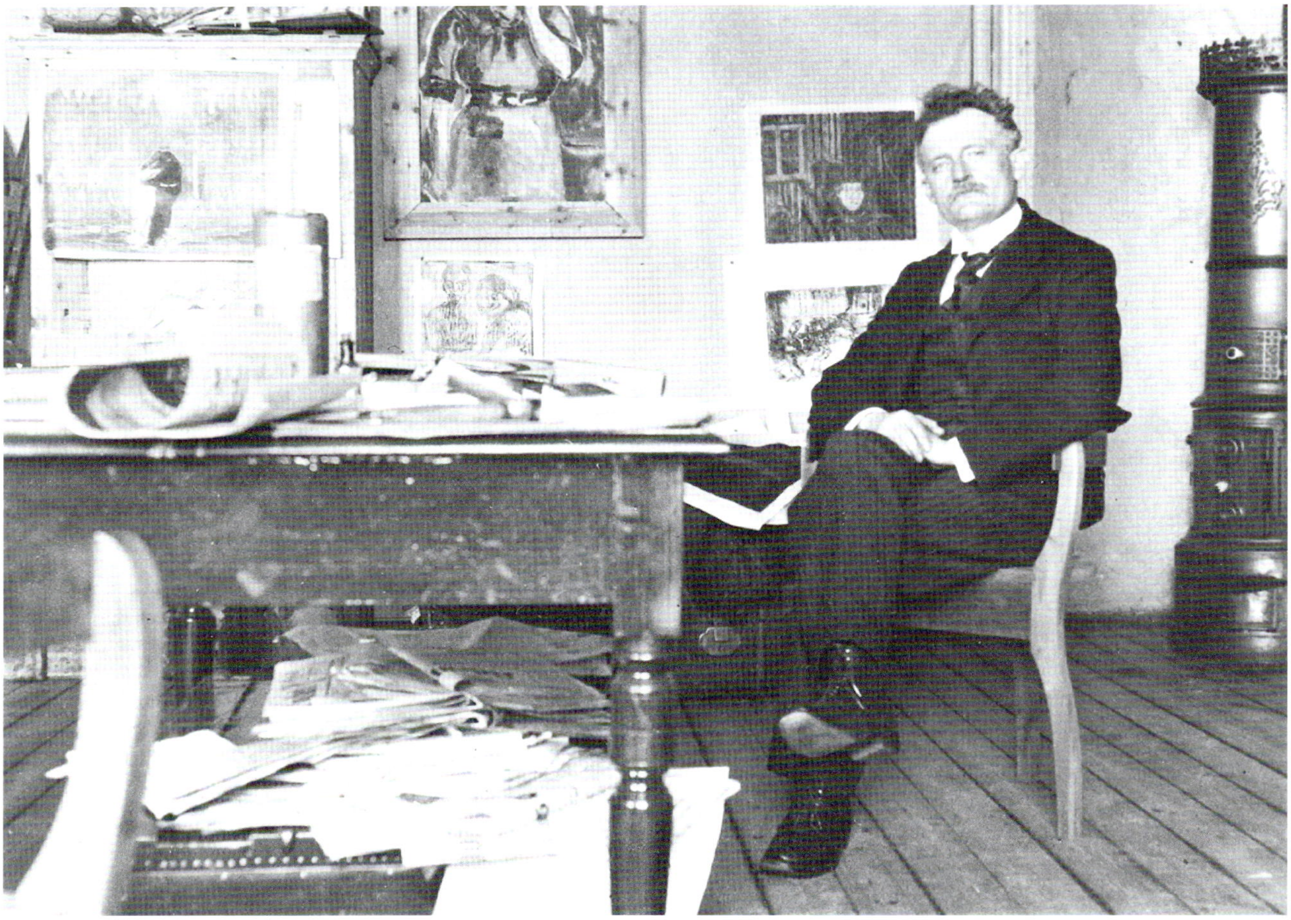

Fig. 7 Munch at Grimsrød manor, c.1913, with the woodcut *Moonlight I* (20) on the wall behind

so on, which are matters best left to experts. At the time, the medium of woodcut was the province mainly of illustrators – especially the polished images of a successful young Swiss artist, Félix Vallotton – Japanese prints, and the then little-known work of a 'natural genius', Paul Gauguin. Munch would make woodcuts in a new and unexpected way, providing, as the historian G.F. Hartlaub identified, an important source of Expressionist printmaking: 'It is the knife of Munch, which in contradiction to all classical idealism and Renaissance taste, first spoke its own peculiar barbaric dialect in rough wood.'[2]

Glaser's remark of 1917 quoted above, however, needs further qualification: Curt Glaser was one of Munch's most important supporters, and as a private collector, art historian and eventually keeper of Berlin's Kupferstichkabinett, he made sure that Berlin's holding of Munch's prints became the most important outside

2 Quoted in Peter Selz, *German Expressionist Painting* (Berkeley: University of California Press, 1957), 81.

Norway.[3] His remark reveals a judgement of the superior quality of the woodcuts among Munch's prints, and his recognition of the strong influence they were having on the work of German artists in the decade in which he wrote. In fact, the artist did not, as suggested, abandon the techniques of etching or lithography when he made his first woodcuts in 1896. Indeed, they remained to the end of his life the techniques he used to make most of his prints. So, as far as prints are concerned, it was principally equipment for making lithographs that Munch's friend Christian Gierløff noticed on his visit to Hvitsten in 1913, amidst a chaos that even Munch himself was not able to navigate:

> He has no less than forty-three studios altogether in his four houses at Kragerø, Ramme, Åsgårdstrand and Grimsrød on Jeløya: all his rooms are studios. He does not possess very much more furniture than he had twenty years ago, when he was a penniless young artist: a few cane chairs are the most luxurious items. His rooms are his workshops, for his pictures, easels, portfolios, lithographic presses, etching tools and electric furnaces are to be found scattered in every room.[4]

For Munch, the woodcuts remained just one part of his output, even though from the time of their making others began to appreciate that they provided the perfect expression of his ideas. At any rate, we can see their numerical significance by looking at Munch's output in the years following his mental breakdown. The decade 1910–19 was his most prolific of all for prints, with a total of 264 new works.[5] A peak in production came during World War I, when Norway experienced a sudden economic growth due to its neutrality: in the two years 1915–16, Munch made 111 new prints, including fifteen woodcut subjects, which, we can surmise, were stimulated by the reprinting at that time of some of the now famous woodcuts of the period 1896–1902. However, the fifteen woodcuts of these two prolific years are greatly outnumbered by

3 See Sigrid Achenbach, *Edvard Munch, Die Graphik im Berliner Kupferstichkabinett* (Berlin: G+H Verlag, 2003).

4 Quoted in J.P. Hodin, *Edvard Munch* (London: Thames & Hudson, 1972), 198–99.

5 Gerd Woll, *Edvard Munch: The Complete Graphic Works* (London: Philip Wilson Publishers; New York: Harry Abrams, 2001), nos. 373–636, 261–381.

21 *Evening. Melancholy I,*
1896, woodcut

One of Munch's earliest woodcuts made in Paris (20, 22), the motif shows a melancholic young man on the shore at Åsgårdstrand, tormented by his lost love. In a later woodcut version of the image (32), we see more clearly the background scene in which three figures prepare to take to a boat from the landing stage. The image was inspired by Munch's own experience, but also by Max Klinger's etching *The Night* (fig. 2) of 1885. The little drama of the departing boat subtly provides an image of the thoughts going through the head of the rejected lover.

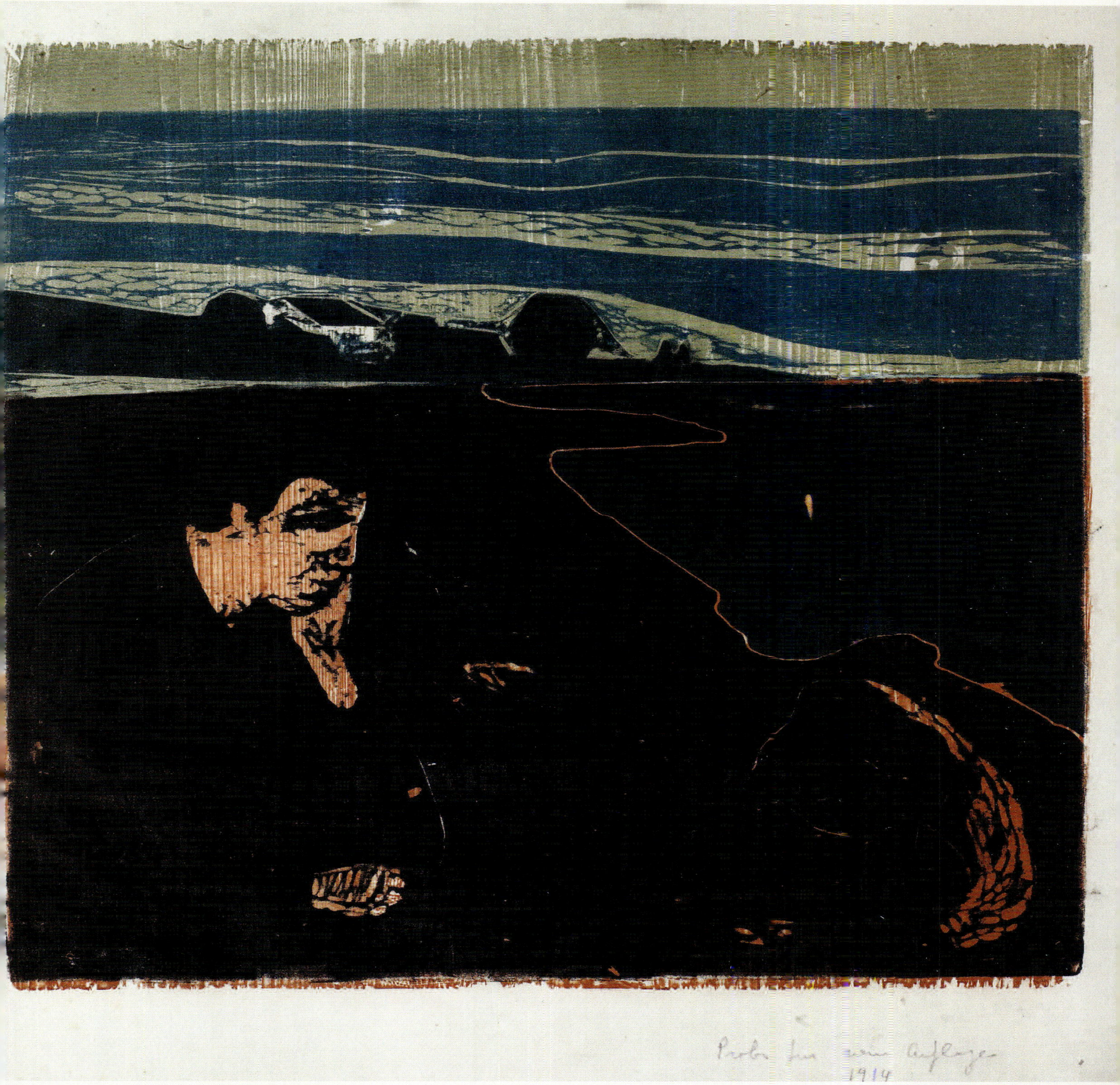
Probe für eine Auflage
1914

the twenty-seven new etchings and sixty-eight lithographs made in the same period.

Munch's first woodcuts were just one part of the burst of activity that took place at the same time as he worked to develop his painted imagery into a monumental cycle. The idea of the frieze first emerged at Munch's Berlin exhibition in 1893, in which a group of works were shown as part of a series that was to be called *Love*. Later, twenty-two paintings made up the cycle that Munch showed in 1902 at the Berlin Sezession, by which time the arrangement of three themes – love, anxiety and death – had been settled. By 1918 the group was known finally as the *Frieze of Life*. Munch's extraordinary activity as a printmaker in this period is clearly related to this major project. Indeed, he worked to organise a group of prints into a portfolio – which was in fact never published – that would have presented his graphic work in the form of such a frieze. Bente Torjusen wrote a seminal article about Munch's prints that focuses on his venture, announced at the Kristiania Diorama exhibition in 1897, to launch just such a portfolio of prints known as *The Mirror*.[6] The portfolio, as reconstructed by Torjusen, consisted of twenty-five prints, including five woodcuts, although the artist thought of the whole as a collection of lithographs. We know this from Munch's correspondence: when he writes home to his aunt of a possible publication in December 1896, just after making his first woodcuts, Munch mentions the portfolio: 'I may publish some lithographs that might earn me some money.'[7]

Munch's first woodcuts printed in colours from multiple blocks, *Moonlight I* (20) and *Evening. Melancholy I* (21), were at first probably printed only in small numbers. That Munch had the idea of printing his woodblocks in several colours from the start seems clear both from the woodcut-like lithograph *Angst* (W. 63), impressions of which are known in black and red inks that have been rolled carefully onto the separate areas of the stone, and from the hand coloured impressions of the woodcuts that were included in *The Mirror*. It seems safe to interpret these as prototypes for subsequent colour printed impressions. Elizabeth Prelinger is con-

6 Bente Torjusen, 'The Mirror', in Robert Rosenblum, Arne Eggum et al., *Edvard Munch: Images & Symbols* (Washington, D. C.: National Gallery of Art, 1978), 185–227.

7 Torjusen, 1978, 192.

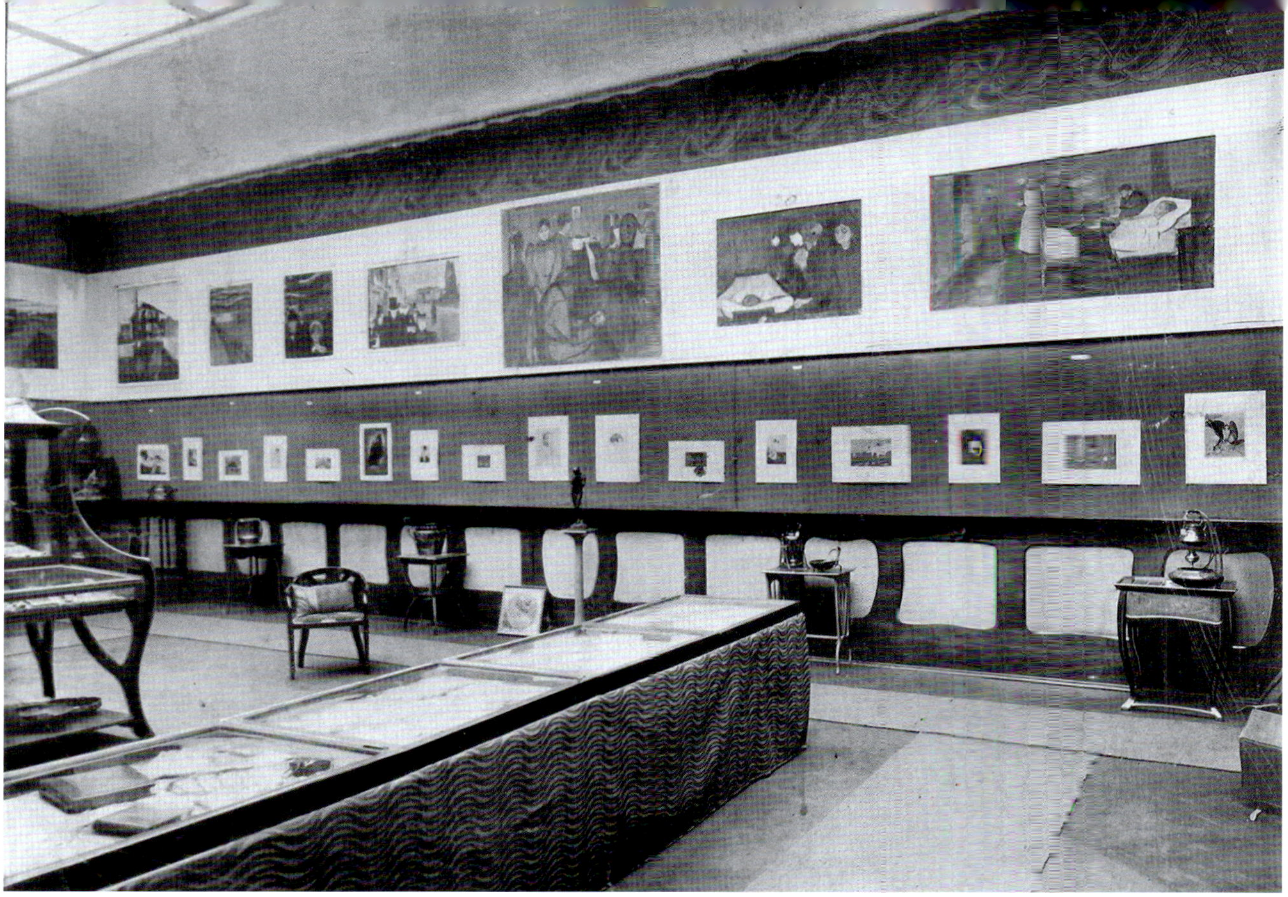

Fig. 8 Exhibition of the *Frieze of Life* at P.H. Beyer & Sohn, Leipzig, 1903, with prints exhibited in frieze below the paintings.

fident that Munch's 'puzzle' method of inking his blocks was in use early, perhaps as early as 1896. She suggests that it may have been the experience of cutting the proofs for *Man's Head in Woman's Hair* (W. 89) to make the cover images for the *The Mirror* portfolio that first gave him the idea.[8] A date by which it is certain that Munch had fully developed his puzzle print process is 1902, the year in which replacement blocks were made for two subjects already cut: *Moonlight I* (20) and *Evening. Melancholy I* (21).[9] As Gerd Woll has suggested, Munch probably assumed that these had been lost in the move of his stones and blocks to Berlin for reprinting in 1902.[10] Prelinger describes the process by which such works as *Melancholy III* (32), the replacement image, were made:

> In his idiosyncratic woodblock method, Munch would cut the blocks into pieces with a fine jigsaw, sometimes both the block bearing most of the drawing, as well as the block mainly carrying the background colour with more or less

8 Elizabeth Prelinger, *Edvard Munch Master Printmaker* (New York: W.W. Norton and Co., 1983), 86.

9 The new prints are to be found at Woll, 2001, cats. 202 and 203, 187–190.

10 See Frances Carey, *Modern Scandinavian Prints* (London: British Museum Publications, 1997), cat. 52, 67.

Fig. 9 Postcard from Karl Schmidt-Rottluff on behalf of the Die Brücke group, 28 October 1906, B2210 (B) A

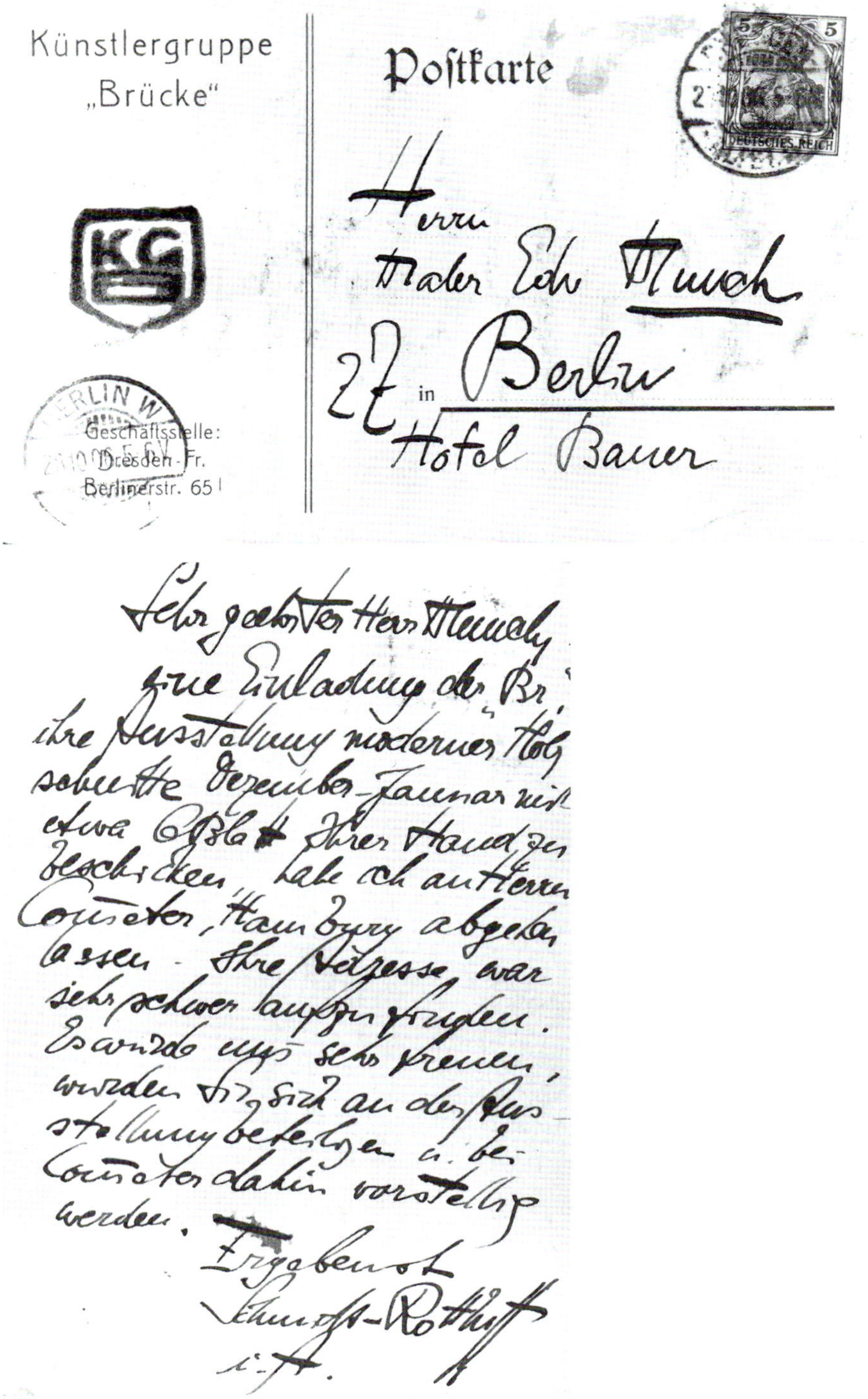

22 *Angst*, 1896, woodcut

Angst is one of Munch's first woodcuts and repeats the image of a lithograph of the same year (W.63). Like *The Scream* (9), Angst is set in countryside with a view of Kristiania fjord, but here we share the anxious individual's view of the faces of passers-by. Their masks echo Ensor's *Christ's Entry into Brussels* (1889), and the swirling sky recalls Van Gogh's landscapes and Gauguin's recent woodcuts. Munch wrote about a rejected lover's feeling of humiliation: 'All the people walking by looked so strange and odd, and he felt as if they were all staring at him, all these faces pale in the evening light' (T.2761).

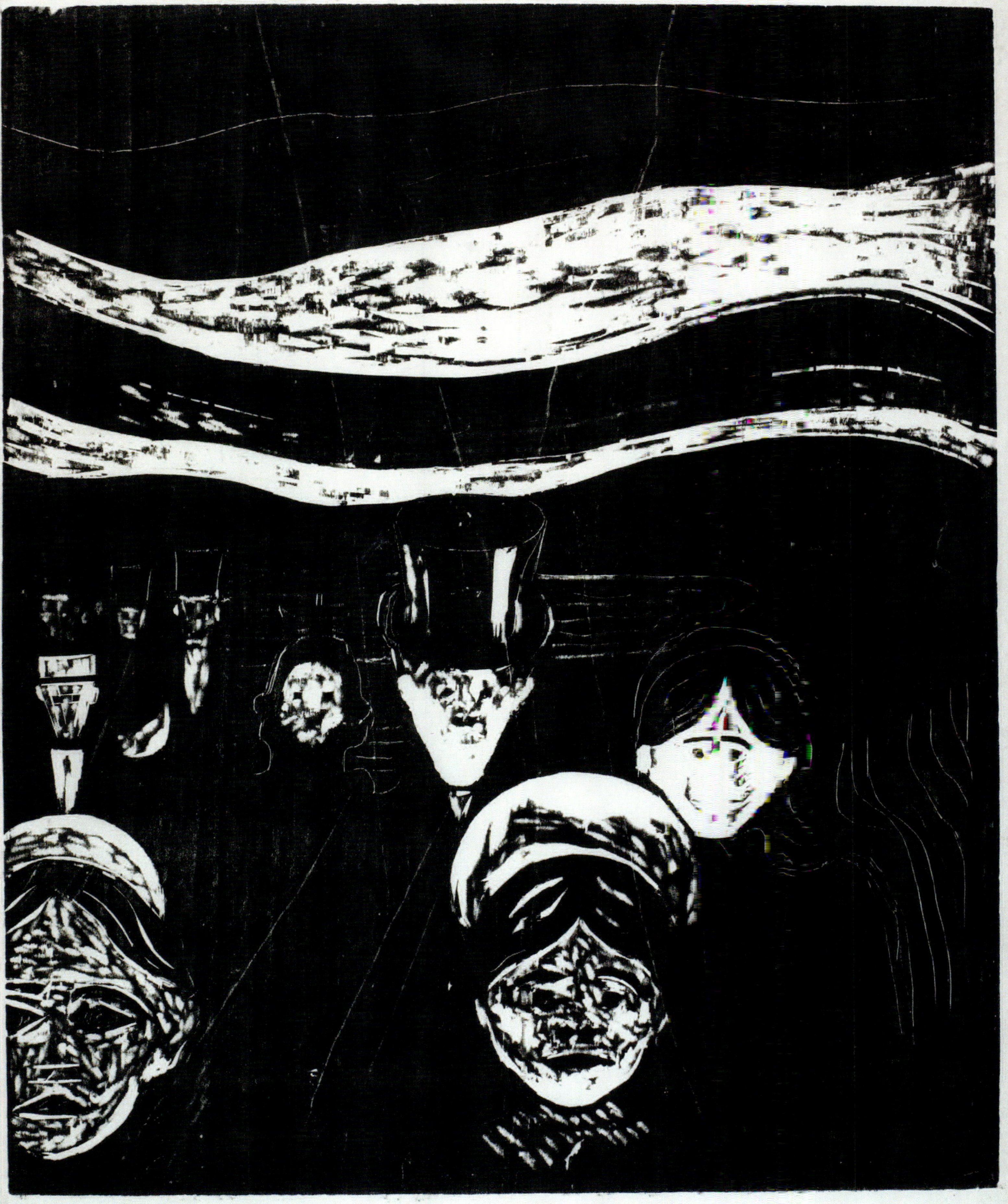

23 *Stéphane Mallarmé*, 1897, lithograph

The poet Mallarmé collaborated with numerous artists. Munch drew this portrait on special 'transfer paper' that is used to impose an image on to a lithographic stone. The epitaph-style inscription with the poet's name resembles Munch's *Self-Portrait* (8), and is modelled on the titles of woodcuts by Gauguin and Vallotton. Munch recorded his reactions to Mallarmé: 'The two eyebrows enormous – and dark – underneath the eyelids a little tired – Two eyes in which the clear day is reflected – the quiet water beneath a bridge - The beard and the hair are grizzled – a little bristly like the beard of a pig'(N 178).

NEXT PAGE

24 *In the Man's Brain*, 1897, woodcut

Man's head is represented as a primitive mask, and above, attached by wavy lines that represent his thoughts, floats the image of a naked woman. Several of Munch's pictures show us, in a separate plane, events that happen in a person's imagination, for example *Jealousy I* (15) and *Melancholy III* (32). *In the Man's Brain* is a more general, totemic statement about man's obsession with woman: the obsession weighs down his spirit. A similar naked woman appears as an 'aura' in the margin of Munch's portrait of *August Strindberg* (14).

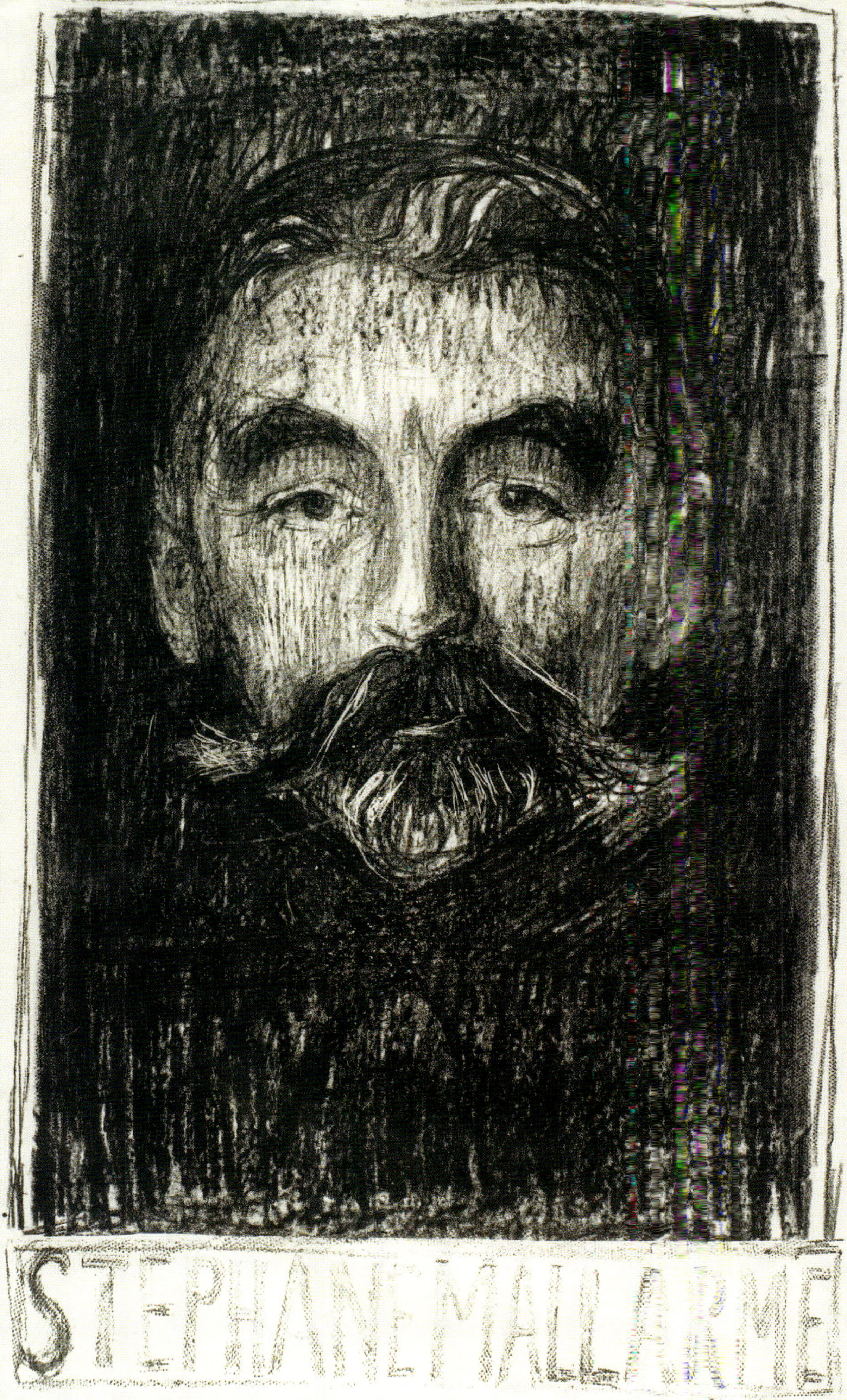
STEPHANE MALLARME

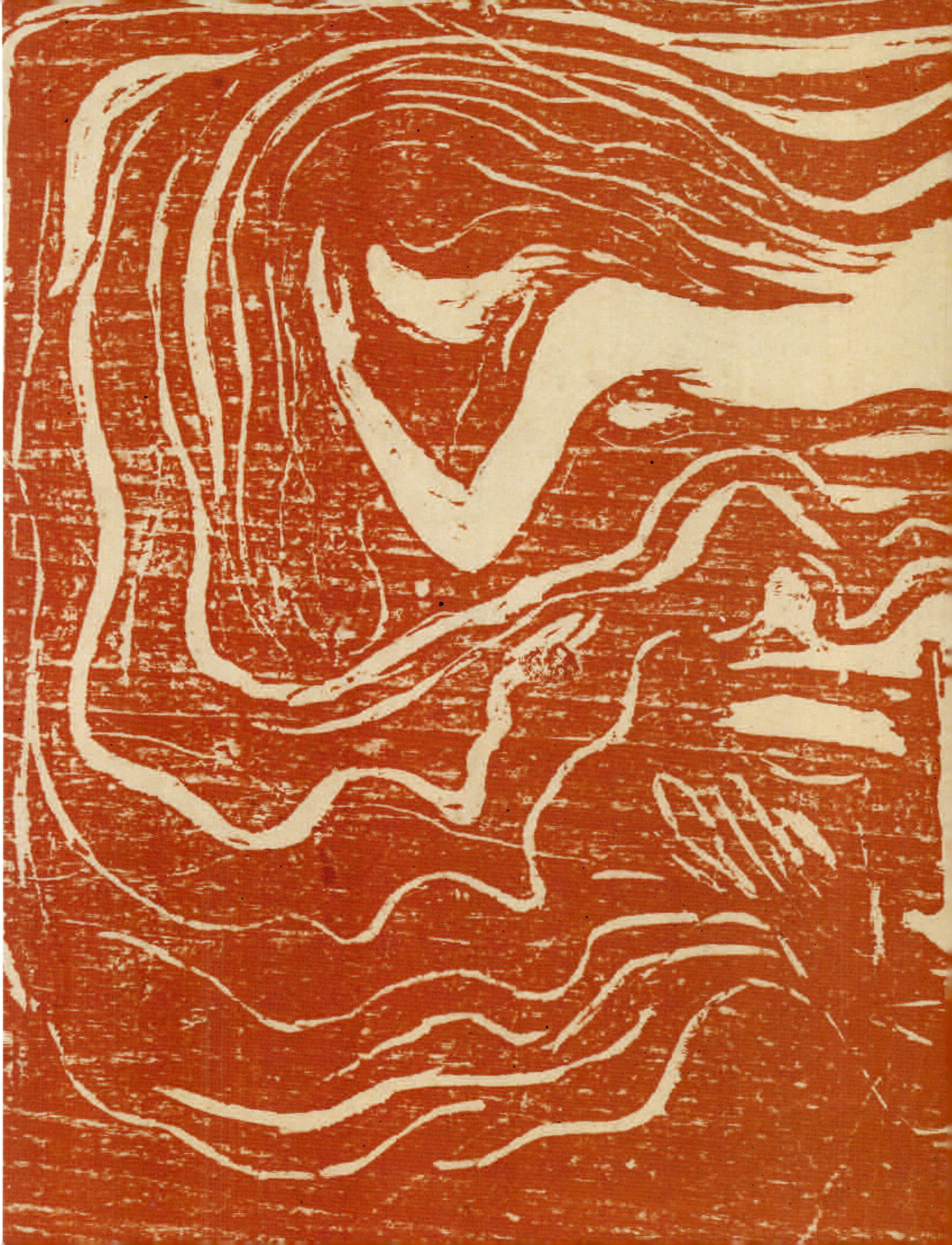

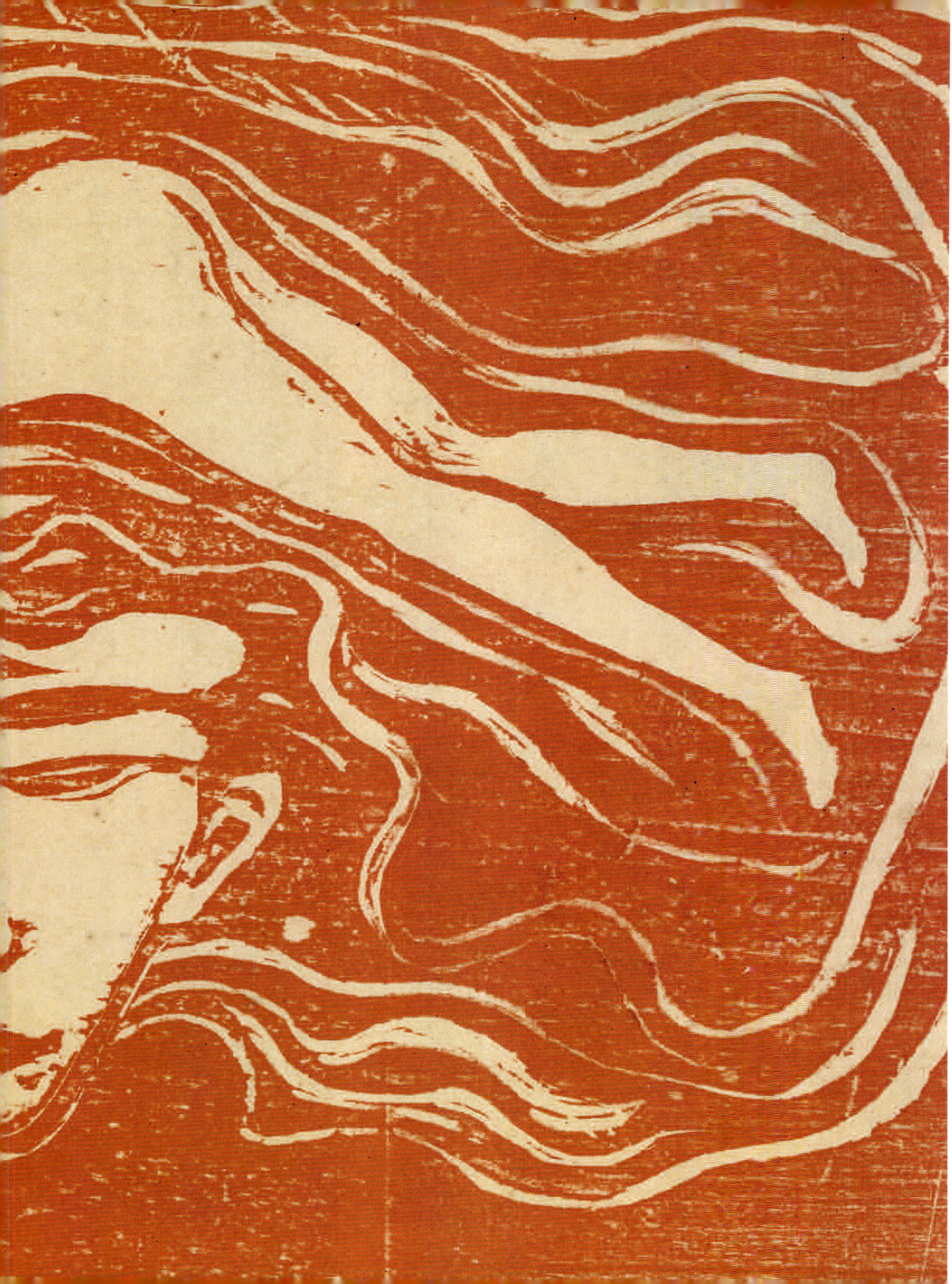

cutting. He would then ink the puzzle-like shapes in different colours, reassemble them and print the variegated surface all at once.[11]

That Munch had created something quite remarkable with his woodcuts of the period 1896–1902 can be glimpsed in some of the responses of critics and artists of the time. When the young artists of the new group Die Brücke organised their first exhibition in Dresden in 1906, Karl Schmidt-Rottluff (1884–1976) was given the task of contacting Munch to persuade him to exhibit his woodcuts along with the work of the group, though a series of letters failed to achieve this end. We also know from the correspondence of the Hamburg judge and print collector Gustav Schiefler (who published the first complete catalogue of Munch's prints in 1907 and was an honorary member of Die Brücke) that Munch's prints deeply impressed the group. Schiefler brought the artists together as best he could, and in 1907, when he showed prints by Munch, he noted Schmidt-Rottluff's interest: 'He looks with great pleasure at the big prints by Munch, and is also interested in Liebermann's etchings.' In a letter of 28 July 1907, Schmidt-Rottluff himself expressed his enthusiasm for the work of Munch, over and above that of Liebermann: 'These Munchs, the two woodcuts and some of the lithographs, are still making a strong impression on me, much more so than the Liebermanns, fine though some of them are. But those Munchs, they were really something!'[12]

The qualities that Munch found and exploited in the woodcuts that so impressed Schmidt-Rottluff were to some extent those that had originally attracted him to lithography in 1895, and which offered several advantages over the intaglio techniques he had previously used: the possibility of larger prints printed in colour and in large editions. When Munch made his first woodcuts, lithography was the medium not only of the *livre illustré*, but of the street poster, and both of these made an impact on his work. There is an interesting interchange between the remote women of Munch's prints of 1895–96 and the seductive, leisured beauties paraded on advertising posters of the period, such as Alphonse Mucha's *Job Cigarettes* (1897). The ecstatic expression of Munch's

25 *Melancholy II*, 1898, woodcut
Melancholy II shows a girl on the Åsgårdstrand shore, with the promontory and lime tree that we know from images such as *Attraction I* (17): she is the female counterpart of the man in *Evening. Melancholy I* (21). Her unhappiness is dramatically emphasised by the contrast between her festive red dress and the black of the shore and sea. Most impressions of this block, which was cut into three pieces to be inked separately, were printed experimentally by Munch himself with a tacky ink that creates atmospheric effects.

11 Elizabeth Prelinger, *Edvard Munch Master Printmaker*, 80.
12 Arne Eggum and Gerd Woll, *Die Brücke – Edvard Munch*, exh. cat. (Oslo: Munch Museum, 1978), 19.

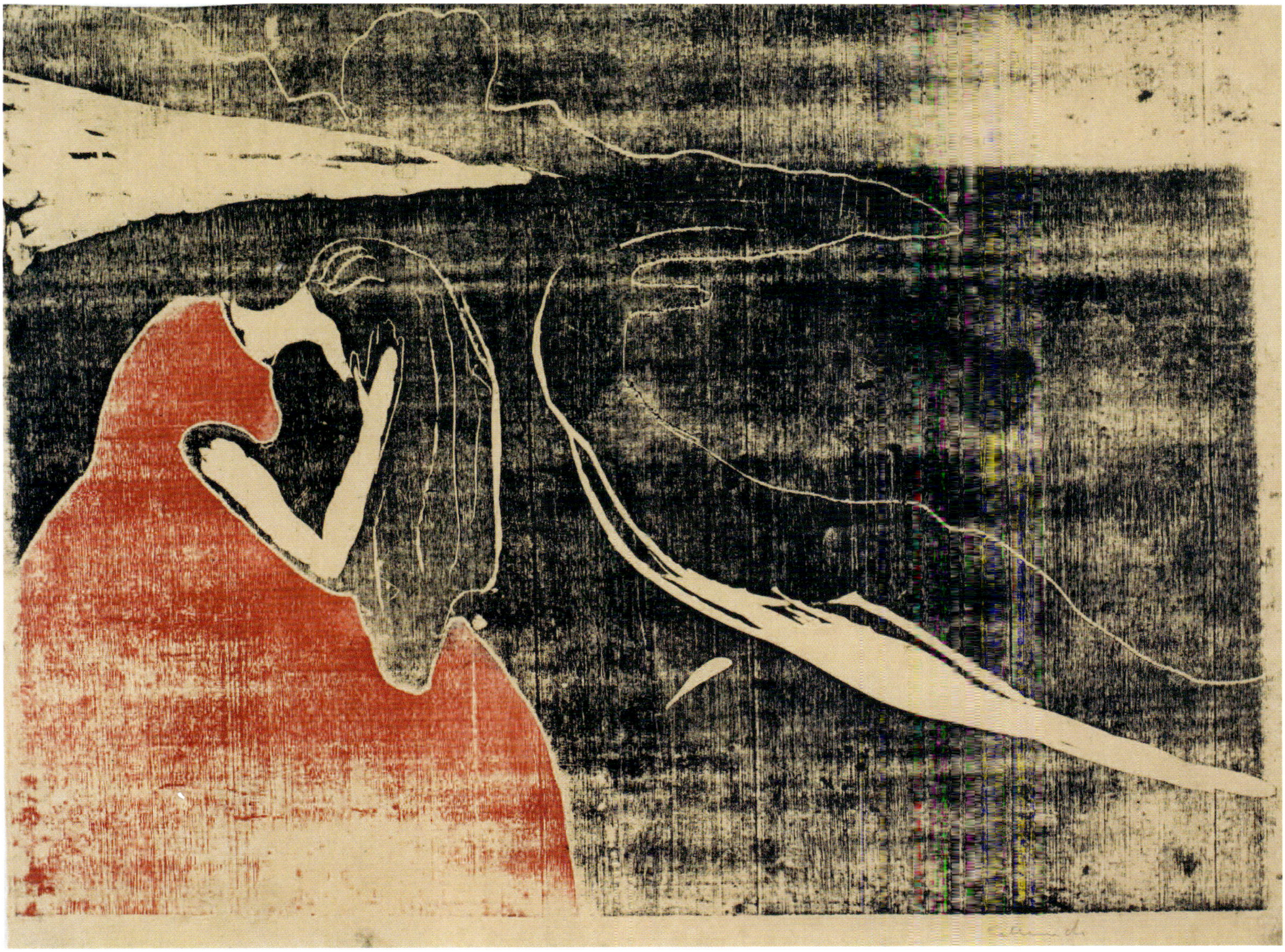

Fig. 10 Cherry woodblock for *Two Women on the Shore* (26), MM P 344

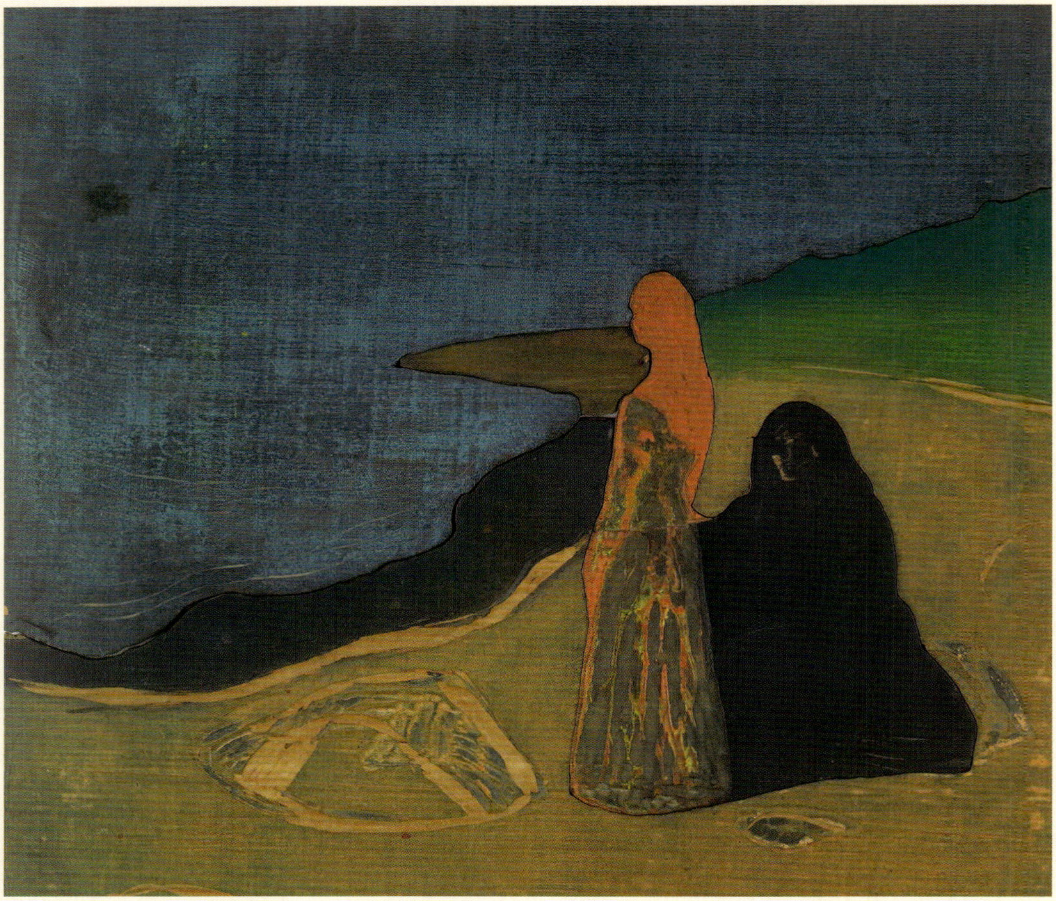

26 *Two Women on the Shore*, 1898, woodcut

Munch was in Paris for the 1896 production of Ibsen's most famous play, *Peer Gynt*. Here Munch's women mirror Ibsen's characters: Peer's old mother Åse and the young Solveig who loves Peer and helps Åse to look for him. Munch noted: 'Down here on the beach I seem to find an image of myself – of my life ... Far, far out there – that soft line where the air meets the sea – it is as incomprehensible as existence' (N 613). In this later impression, typical of the artist's own printing during World War I, Munch added foreground rocks, and inserted the column of moonlight using a paper stencil.

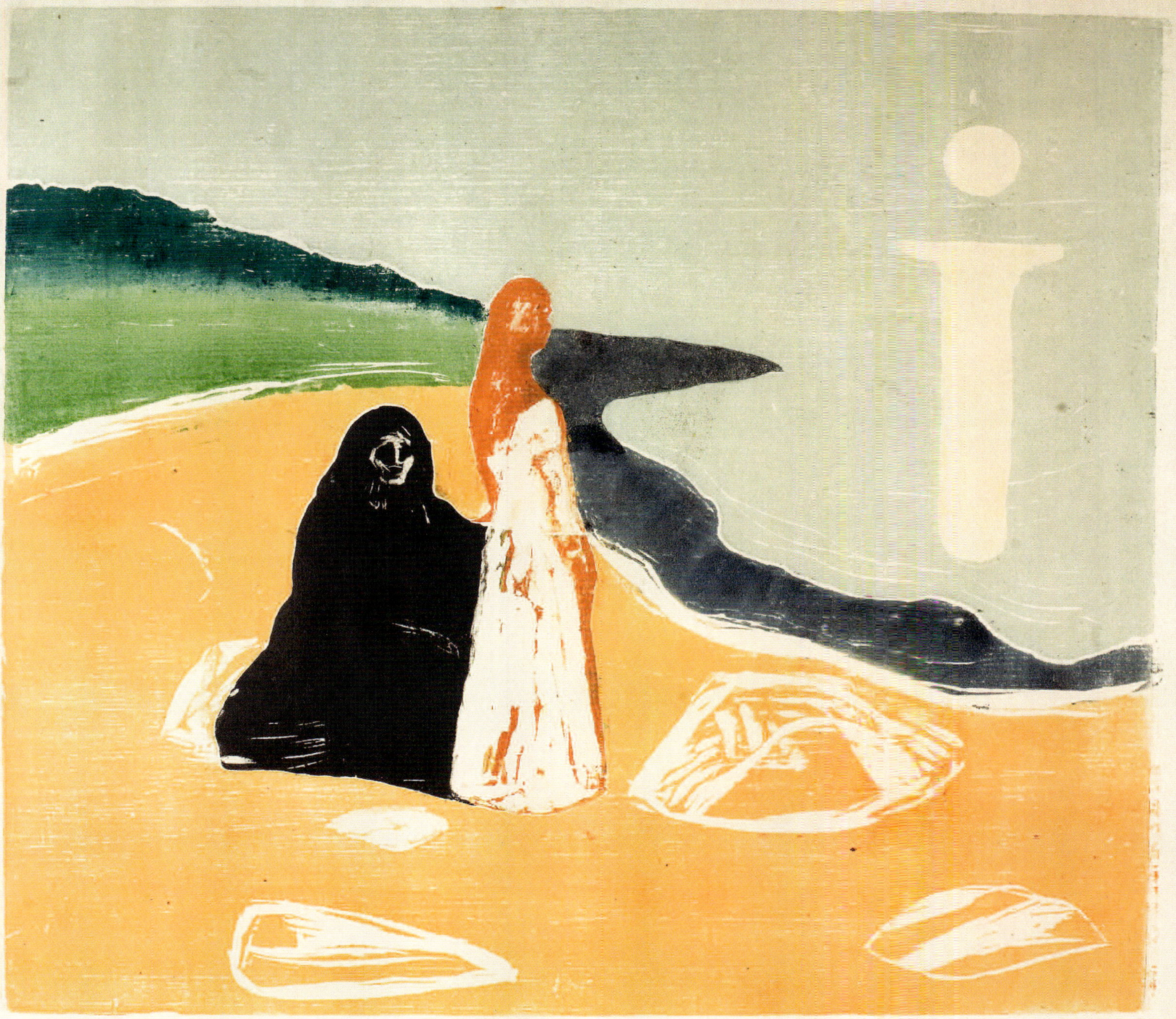

27 *Ashes II*, 1899, lithograph

Ashes is one of the important images of the Love section of Munch's *Frieze of Life*, and it is based on the painting of 1894 in the National Gallery in Oslo. It presents self-loathing and despair in the man, following the consummation of the lovers' physical relationship: presumably the image refers to the extinction of the flame of love in the man, and his anxiety about the woman's sexuality. Commentators have seen a self-portrait in the cowed man. This print is a simplified version of an earlier lithograph (W. 79), which is dominated by a woman's head within a symbolic border.

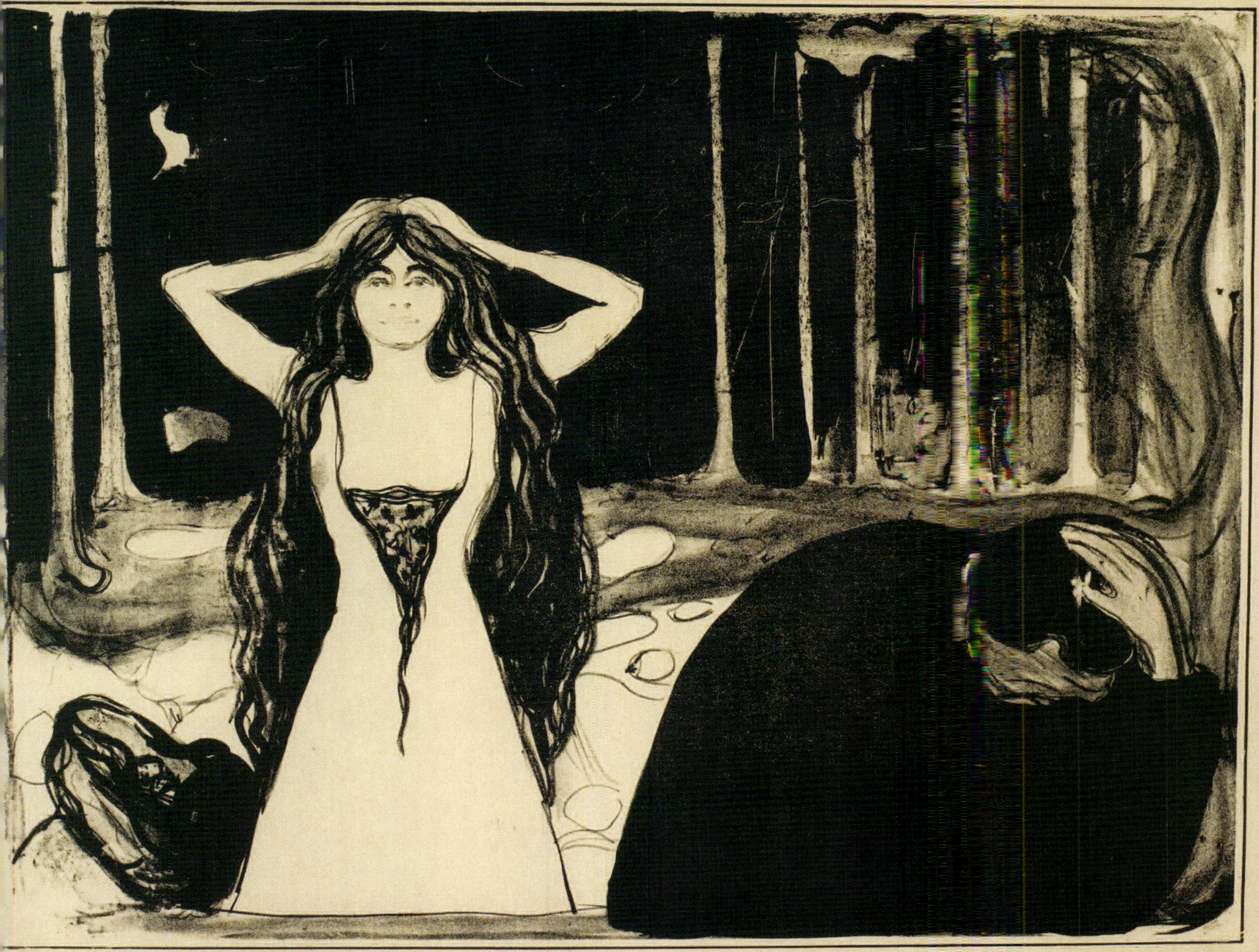

Fig. 11 Jan Toorop, *Delft Salad Dressing*, 1897, lithograph, Rijksmuseum, Amsterdam

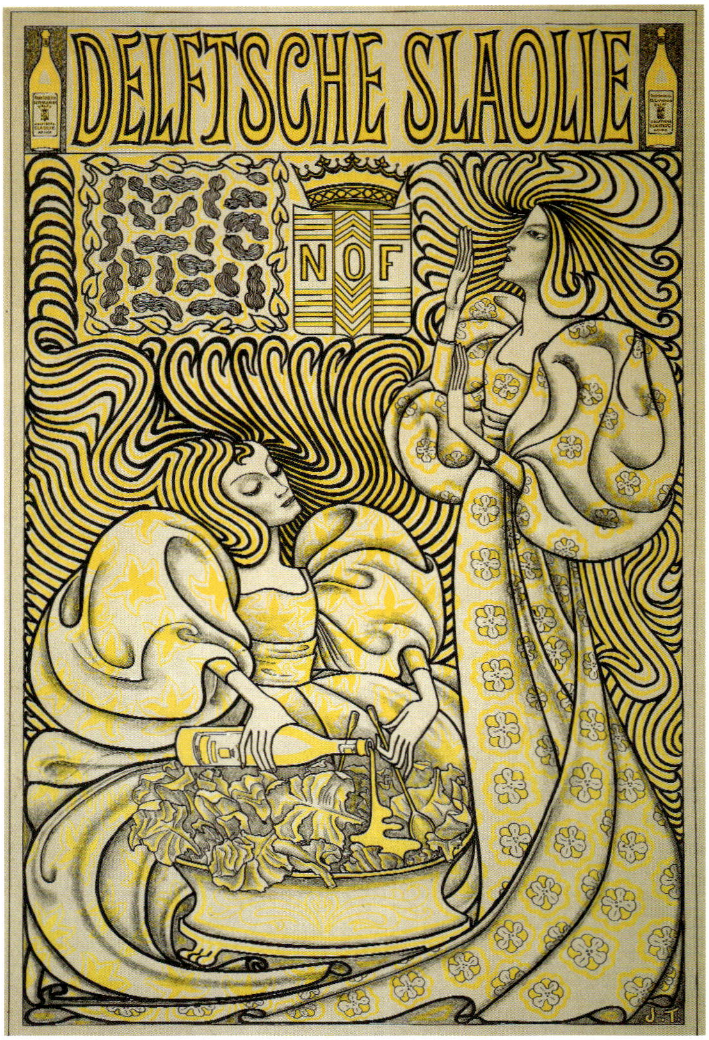

Madonna (10) mirrors those found on any number of posters, advertising things such as cigarettes, bicycles or olive oil, as in Jan Toorop's *Delft Salad Dressing* poster of c.1897 (fig. 11). In some ways, Munch's allegorical world, the Åsgårdstrand shore peopled by lovers, glimpsed in works such as *Attraction I* (17) and *Separation II* (18), has several elements in common with that of Toorop's poster. Here, as in Munch's work, the women's hair swirls out around them in a characteristically Art-Nouveau pattern, like fishing nets used to ensnare men. But perhaps the most influential aspect of the eye-catching advertising imagery was its use of colour: the large paper surfaces of posters inclined artists such as Munch towards the use of flat areas of colour, analogous to and partly inspired by the Japanese woodcuts that became common currency following the *Exposition de la gravure japonaise* at the Ecole des Beaux-Arts in 1890.

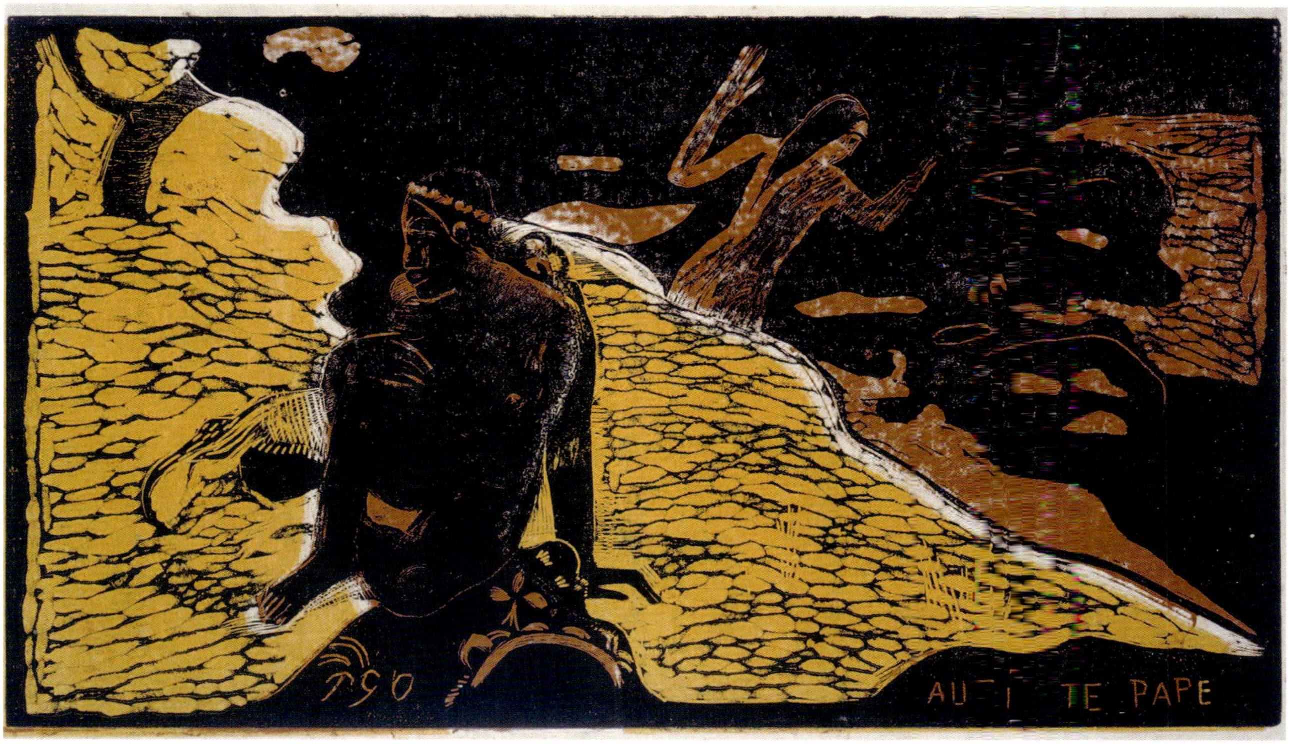

Fig. 12 Paul Gauguin, *The Fresh Water is in Motion*, c.1893–95, woodcut, Albert Roullier Memorial Collection, 1926.27, The Art Institute of Chicago, photography © The Art Institute of Chicago

There are also similarities to be observed between the work of Munch and that of the Japanese woodblock artists, as well as Gauguin, who was influenced by them. Technically speaking, neither the Japanese woodblock artists nor Gauguin could be said to have worked in Munch's 'peculiar barbaric dialect in rough wood', but, like him, they did work in a manner that revealed the character of the material. In Gauguin, as in Japanese prints, we see the imprint of the wood grain, an aspect that Munch developed into an important expressive tool. His woodcuts, such as *Two Human Beings. The Lonely Ones* (29) or *The Kiss IV* (33), reveal the images as if they have been found inside the wood. The grain is familiar to us as a measure of the growth and aging of wood, and unconsciously it becomes a part of an image about the passage of humans through life.

The exact chronology of Munch's woodcuts is hard to pin down, and the facts are obscured by his unfulfilled struggle over the period 1897–1902 to publish a portfolio of prints. Almost all of Munch's most important prints were made within the crucial period of 1893–1902, in which the frieze idea edged towards its final form. The idea of publishing a portfolio, which Torjusen has reconstructed, makes perfect sense alongside Munch's campaign to promote his art, not as small paintings in large frames of the kind that dealers found easy to dispose of, but as part of a notional public

Fig. 13 One of two woodblocks for *Woman's Head against the Shore* (28), M M P 356

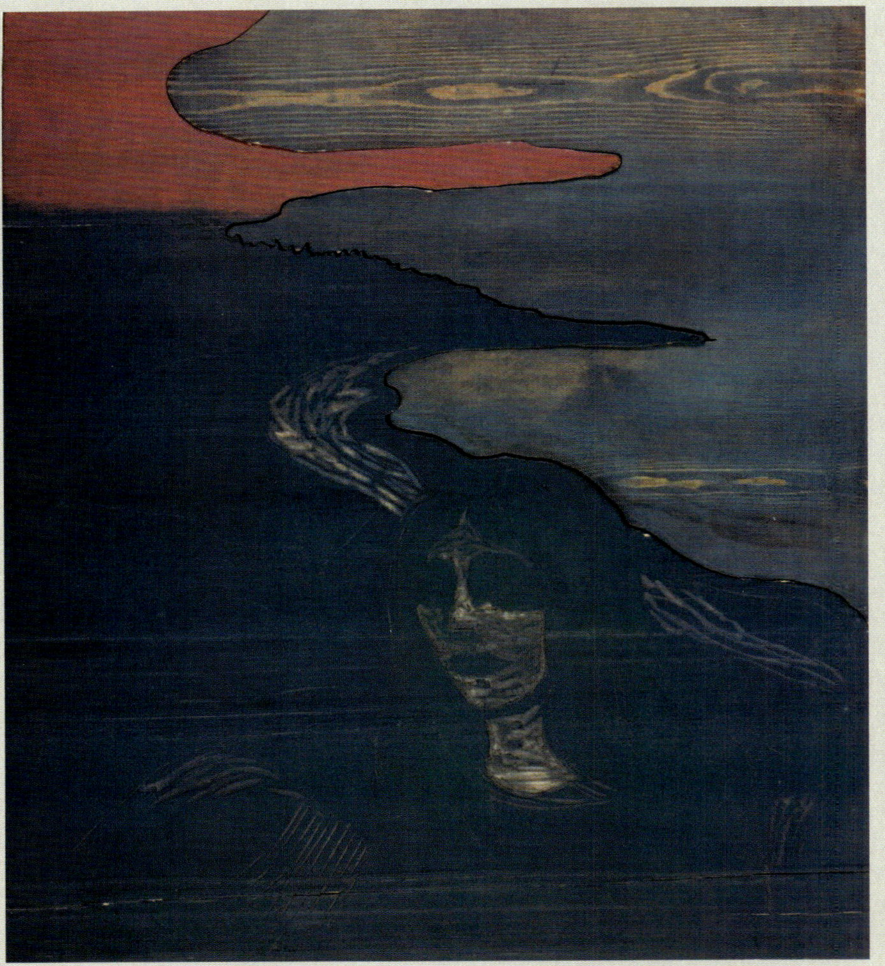

28 *Woman's Head against the Shore*, 1899, woodcut

Rather like a Renaissance artist who follows traditional figures used by his workshop, Munch repeats his own successful motifs, especially the images of man and woman against the Åsgårdstrand shoreline. This woman's head, turning away from the vastness of the sea, resembles the heavy-eyed widow with bowed head, who represents the third stage of life in the earlier etching *Woman II* (7). One of the two blocks used for printing is reproduced on this page.

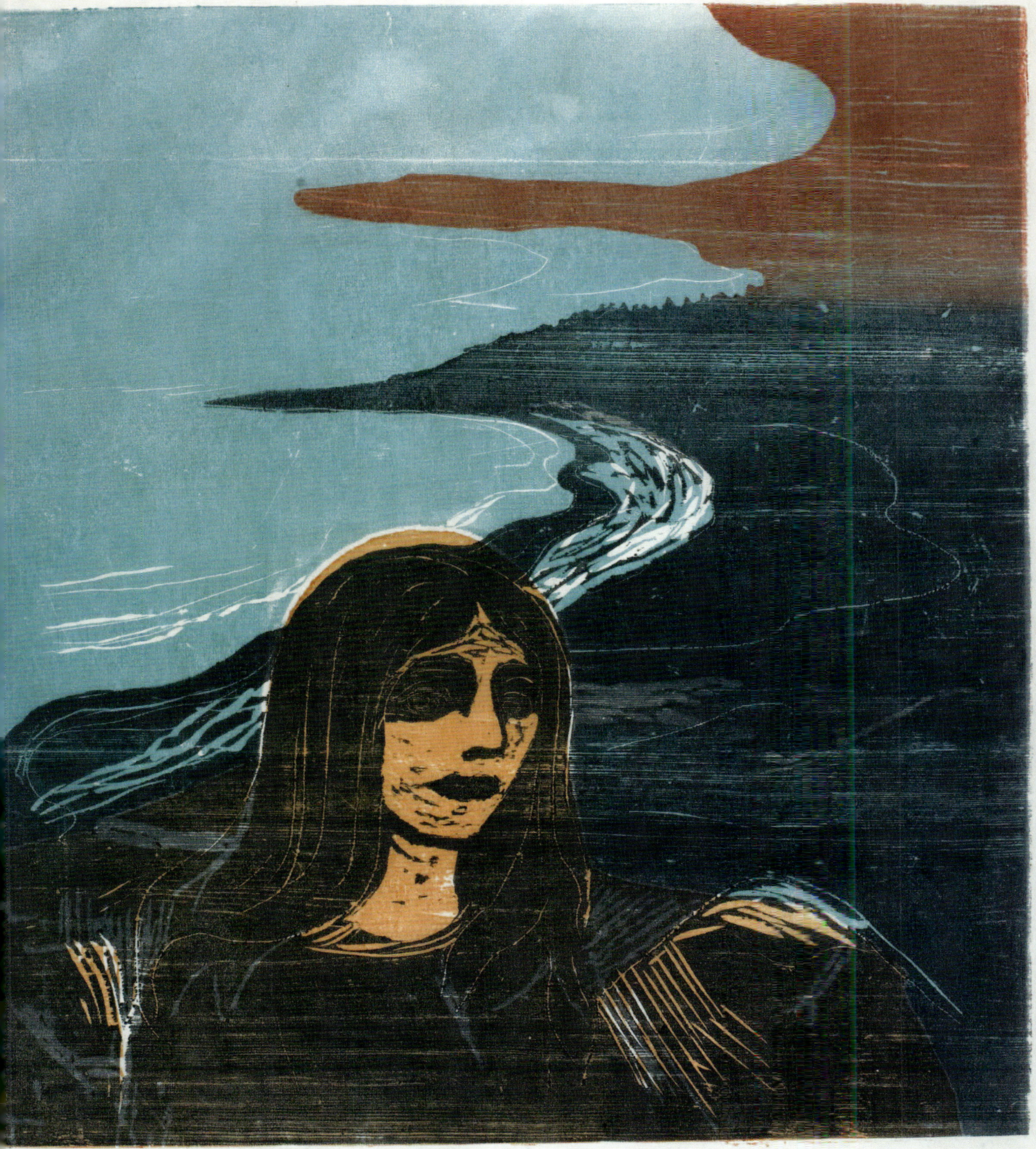

29 *Two Human Beings. The Lonely Ones,* 1899, woodcut

Two Human Beings. The Lonely Ones repeats the image of one of Munch's drypoints of the 1895 Meier-Graefe portfolio (W. 13). It presents man and woman on the shore, staring outwards together. The stronger colour medium of the woodcut makes the symbolism of this version more powerful. In their attitudes we see how differently man and woman respond to the vastness of the sea. In this impression the column of moonlight separates them and emphasises the emotional distance between them.

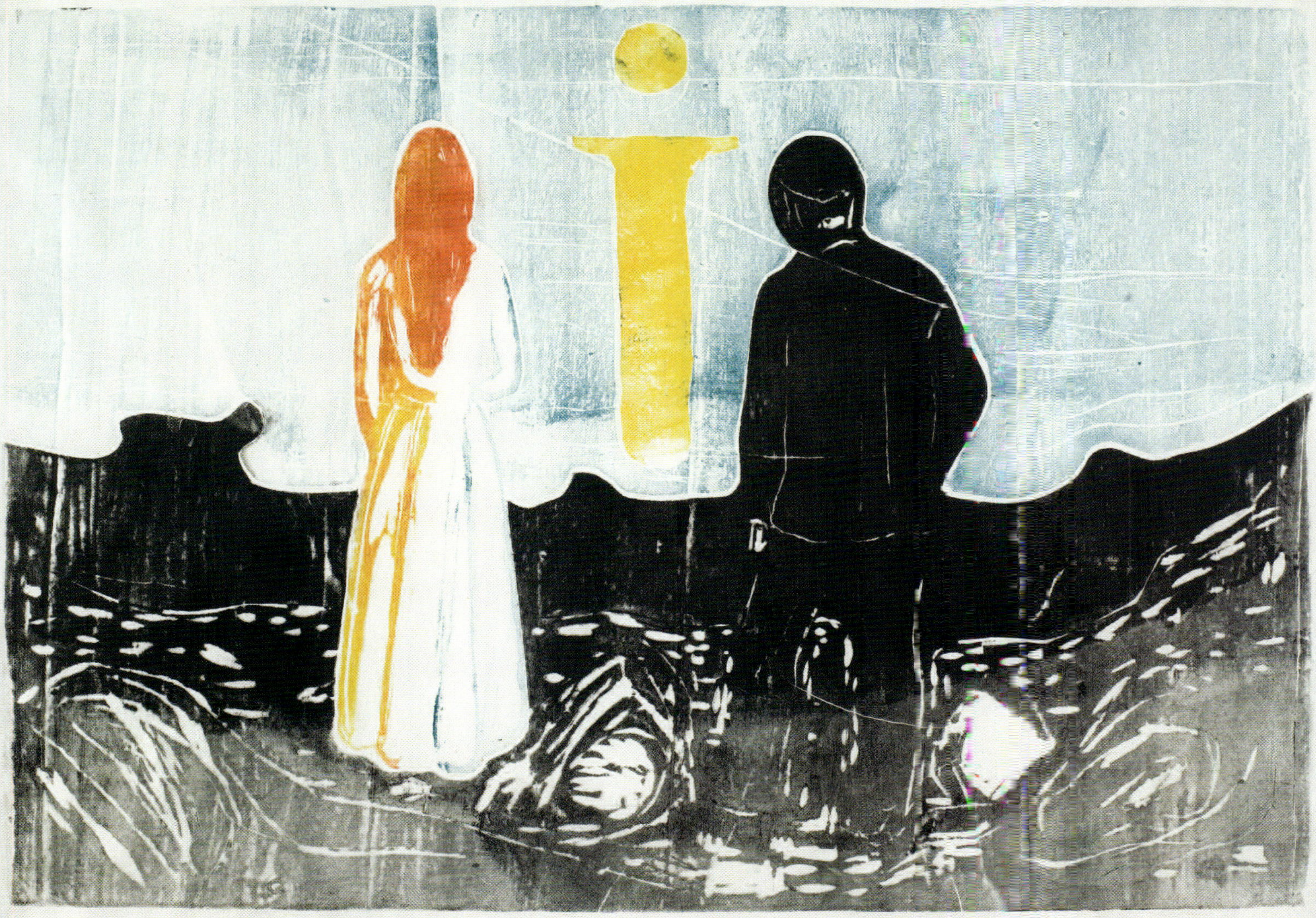

Fig. 14 Photograph of a model in Munch's studio, who resembles the *Woman with Red Hair and Green Eyes. The Sin*, B 2927 (F)

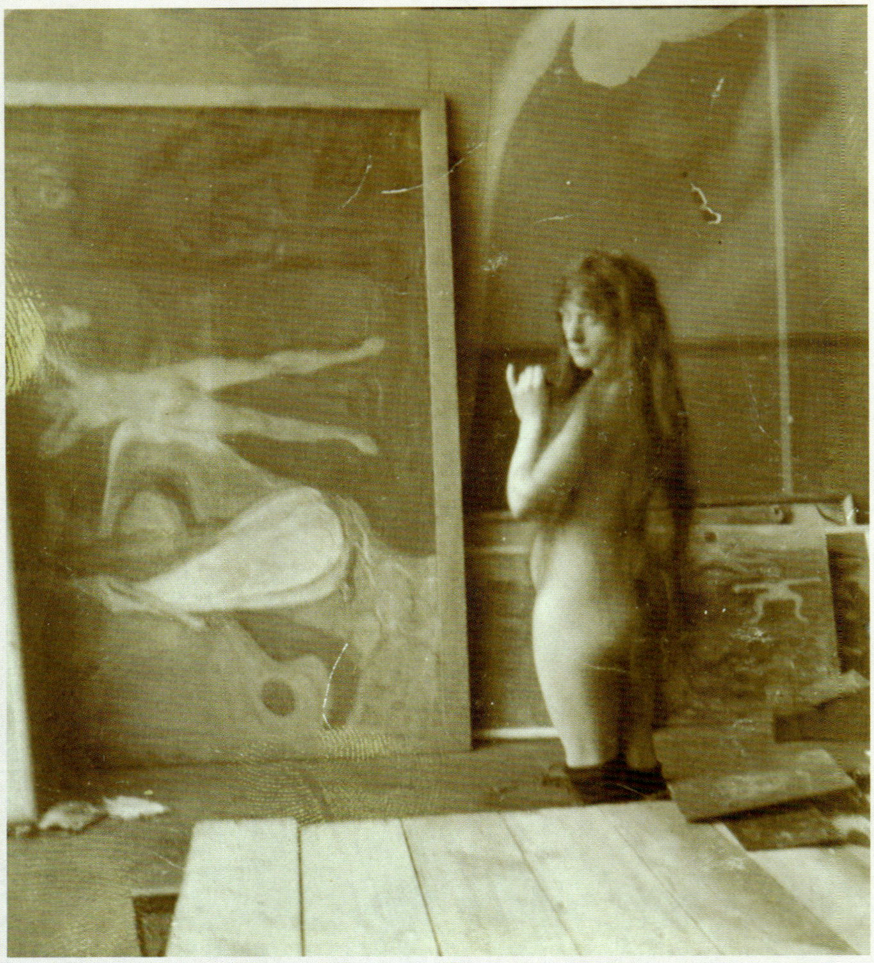

30 *Woman with Red Hair and Green Eyes. The Sin*, 1902, lithograph

Munch often presents women as mysterious beings, and the power they exercised over him is often bound up in their long hair. This red-haired temptress figure, her searing green eyes touched in on the print with blue ink on the printer's finger, is based on one of the artist's photographs (MM B 2927 [F]) showing a model in his studio. The print exhibited is a late printing, with added initial letters 'E. T.', which possibly stand for 'Eget Trykk', meaning 'own', or 'artist's proof'.

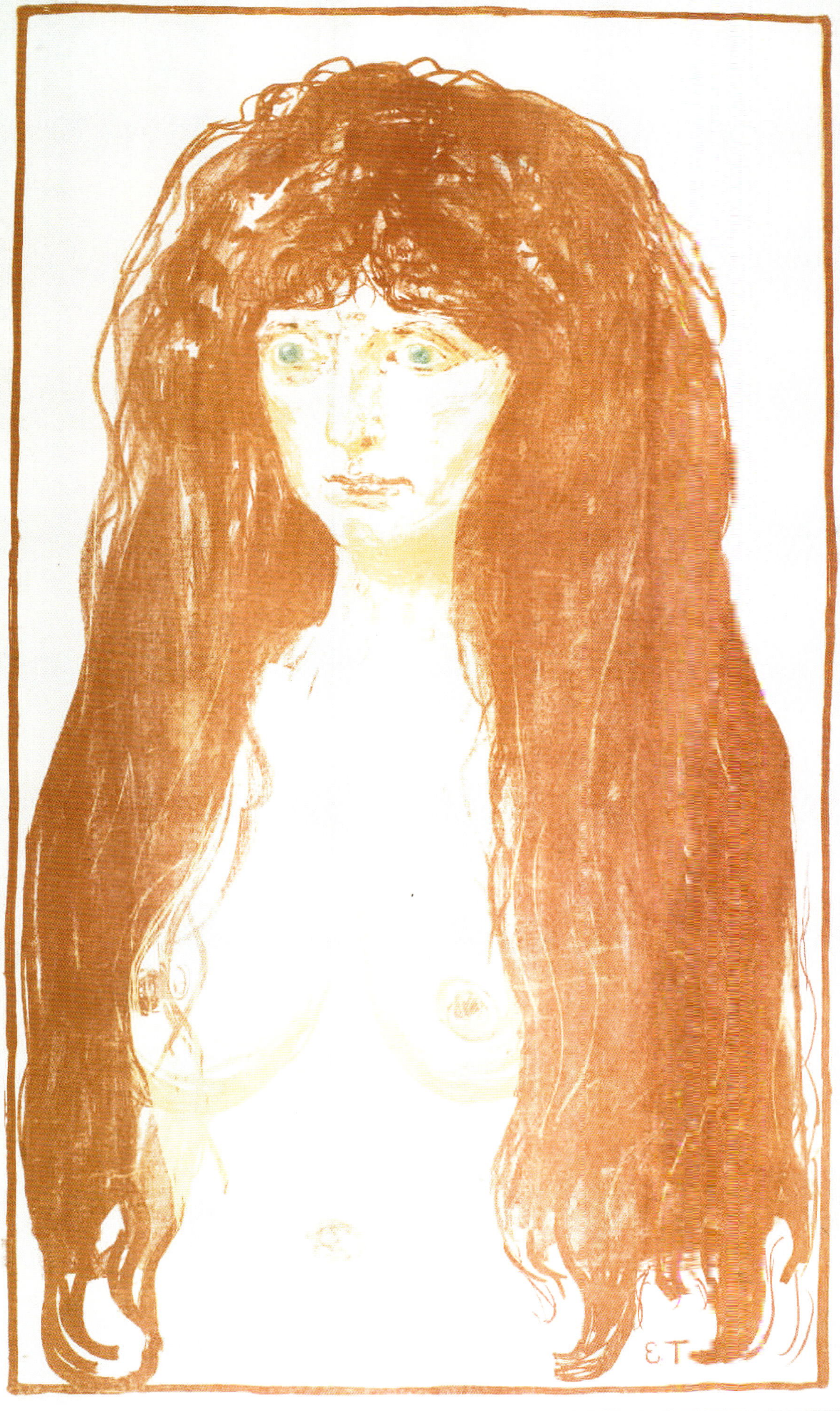

monument. In a similar way, he may have intended the prints to provide near universal access to the imagery of the frieze cycle.

In particular, the terminus post quem for a chronology of the woodcuts is difficult to establish because Munch does not frequently mention his woodcuts and, in addition to this, the surviving impressions of the two earliest works, *Moonlight I* and *Evening. Melancholy I*, mostly date from the early 1900s. The early impressions of these prints listed in the catalogue of the 1897 Kristiania Diorama exhibition are described as hand coloured, which implies that Munch had not yet made an additional block or blocks with which to print in colour. Also that year, we have an intriguing letter from Munch in Paris to Julius Meier-Graefe indicating that he was then using lithographic stones to add colour, in order to make hybrid prints: 'I am at work on various woodcuts – and will – soon send you some of them – If you're to have coloured woodcuts they will have to be printed here – as I am having the colour printed with lithographic stones.'[13] Then in 1902 he organised the transport to Berlin of a large number of his stones and woodblocks to begin a campaign of printing, possibly prompted by his show that year at the Berlin Sezession. 1902 was one of the artist's most prodigious years, with a total of sixty new prints, the bulk of which were etchings (forty-four), but which also included the new versions of the earlier woodcuts, *Moonlight I* and *Evening. Melancholy I*.

In every age the woodcut has a special, direct appeal, and as a result the woodcuts of an artist can sometimes attract what seems to be a disproportionate amount of attention. So, to cite the example of an English Bohemian, whose work appealed to Munch because of his devotion to the idea of a progress, which was mirrored by his own frieze, William Hogarth had two woodcuts made in 1750 for a projected series entitled *Four Stages of Cruelty*. Because of their superior clarity, these prints, although not cut by Hogarth, are always preferred by historians to the artist's own en

gravings of the same subjects when illustrating the 'Age of Morality'. So, Munch's woodcuts of men and women who stand on the Åsgårdstrand shore seem to us archetypal, and more powerful than other versions in which he processed the same ideas, because of the brutal simplification of the image that results when an artist cuts or gouges the wood.

31 *Henrik Ibsen at the Grand Café*, 1902, lithograph

Ibsen's plays were enormously influential in late nineteenth-century Europe. He introduced Scandinavian culture to Europe, paving the way for artists like Munch. Munch met Ibsen (1828–1906) in 1891 at the Grand Café in Kristiania, and this lithograph is based on his memory of that meeting. Ibsen was also interested in Munch, visiting his exhibition in Kristiania in 1895. Munch noted that they 'looked at the pictures together – He studied them carefully – he was particularly interested in the three women [*Woman in Three Stages*]… He was also interested in the man sitting by the sea, cowed and hunched' (T 2759).

13 Torjusen, 1978, 189.

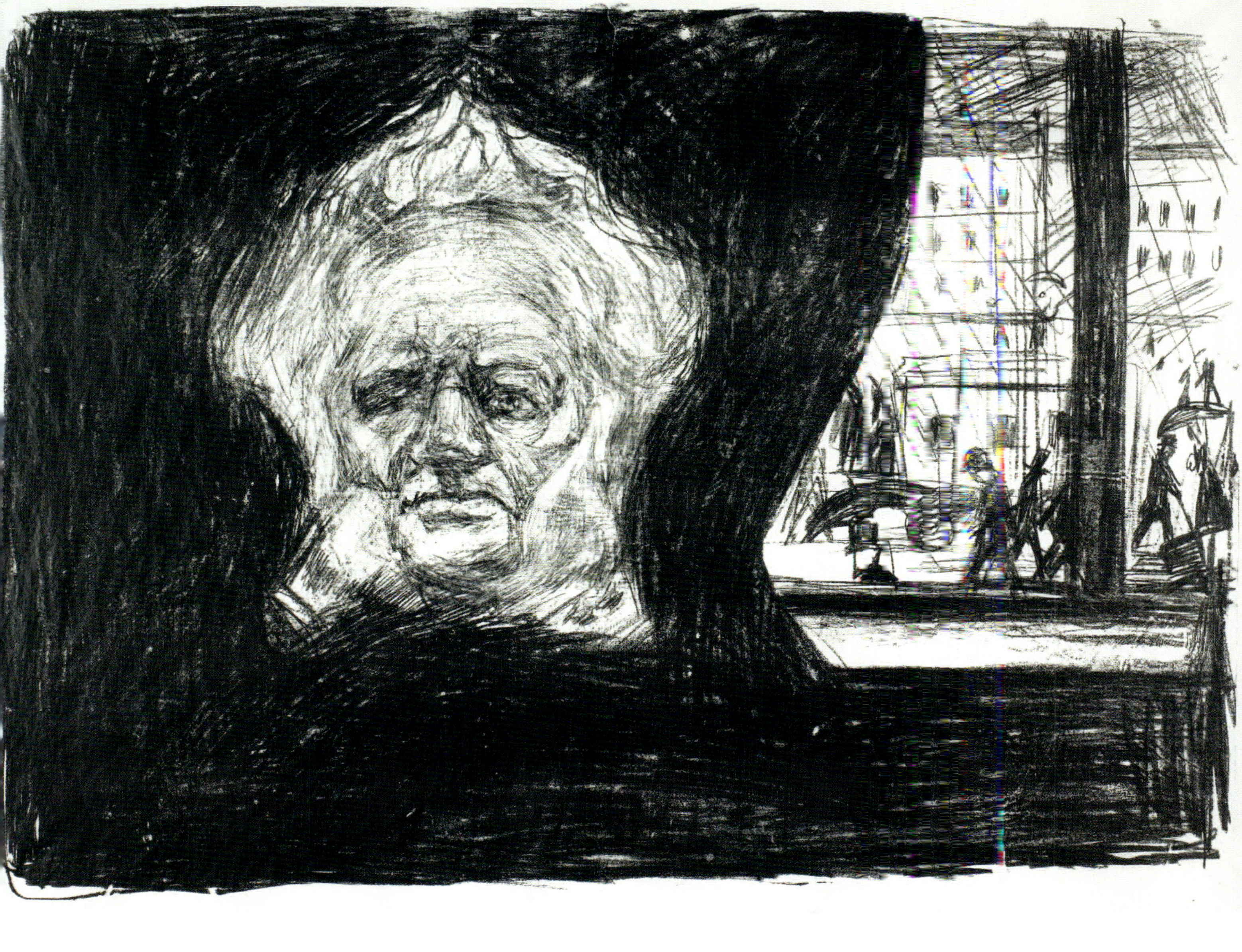

Melancholy, 1894–96, oil on canvas, Munch Museum, PEO 473

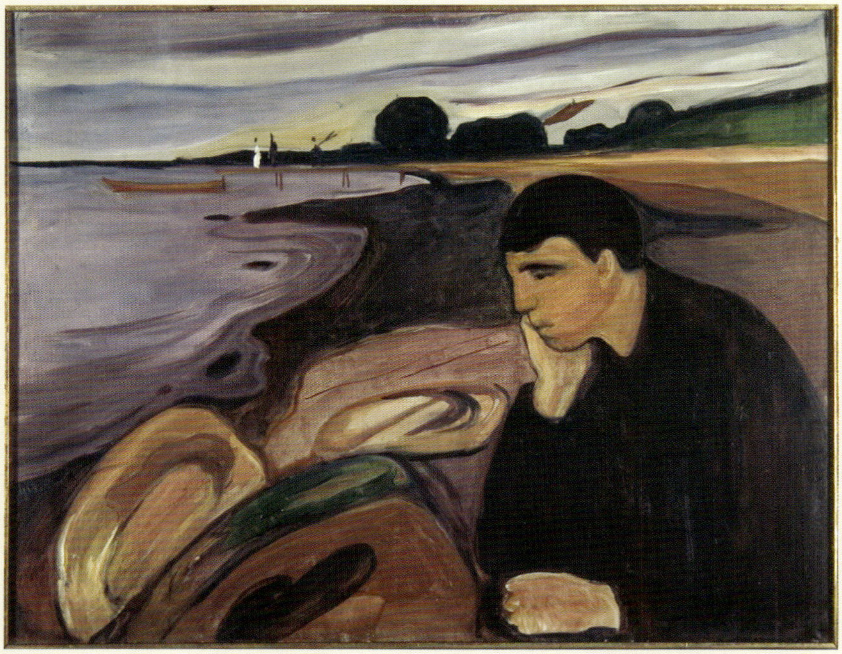

32 *Melancholy III*, 1902, woodcut

Melancholy III is perhaps Munch's most powerful statement of the anxiety of a rejected lover. A young man sits on the shore at Åsgårdstrand: we witness the drama in his imagination, in which three people are about to take to the boat tied to the jetty behind. Munch noted that his friend the art critic Jappe Nilssen modelled for the image, as well as that he personally identified with the young man's situation: 'And the boat was tied up down there – ready to leave. She resembles her. I felt it as a stabbing pain in my chest – if only she were here now' (N 664).

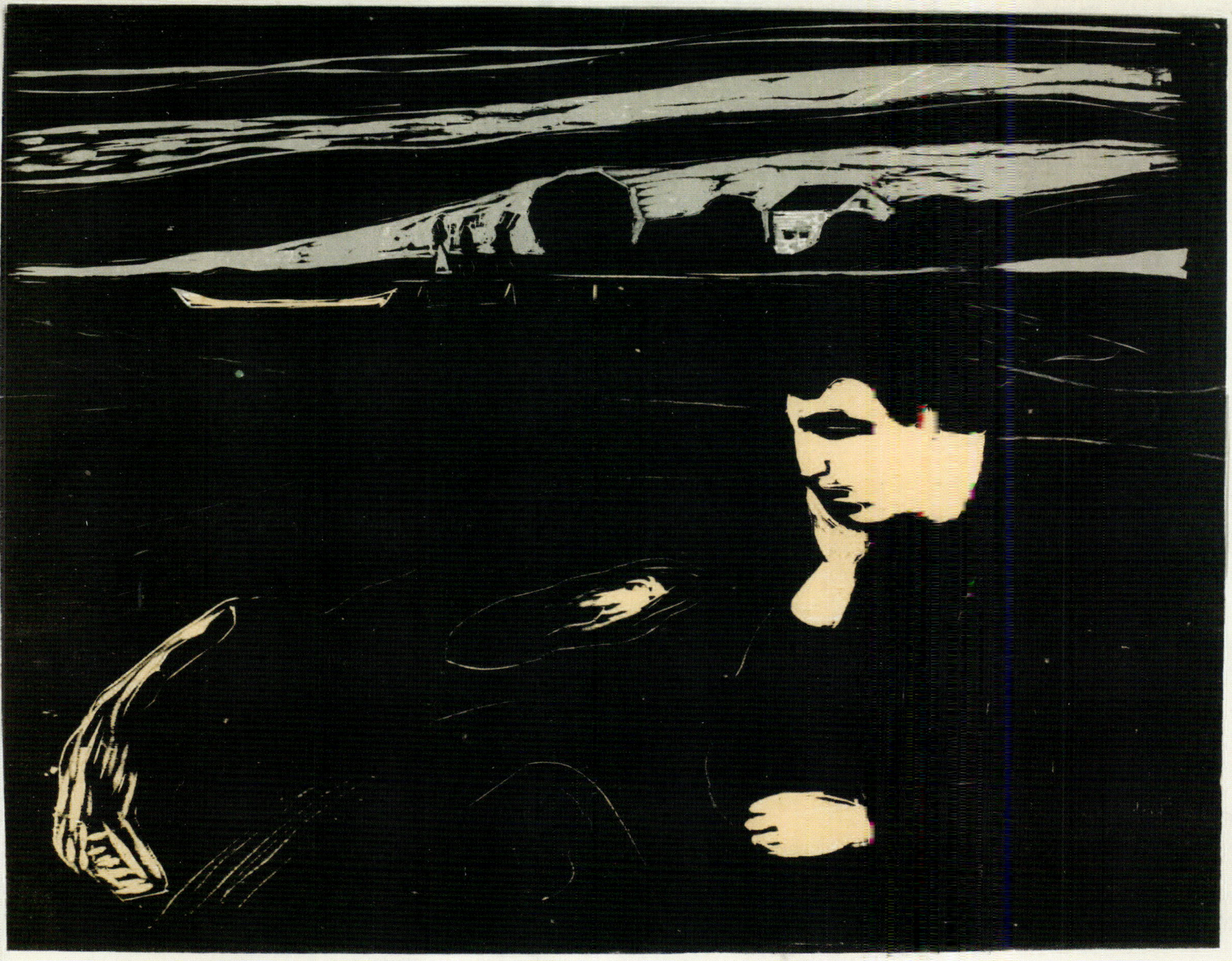

Fig. 15 Woodblock for *The Kiss IV* (33), MM P 336

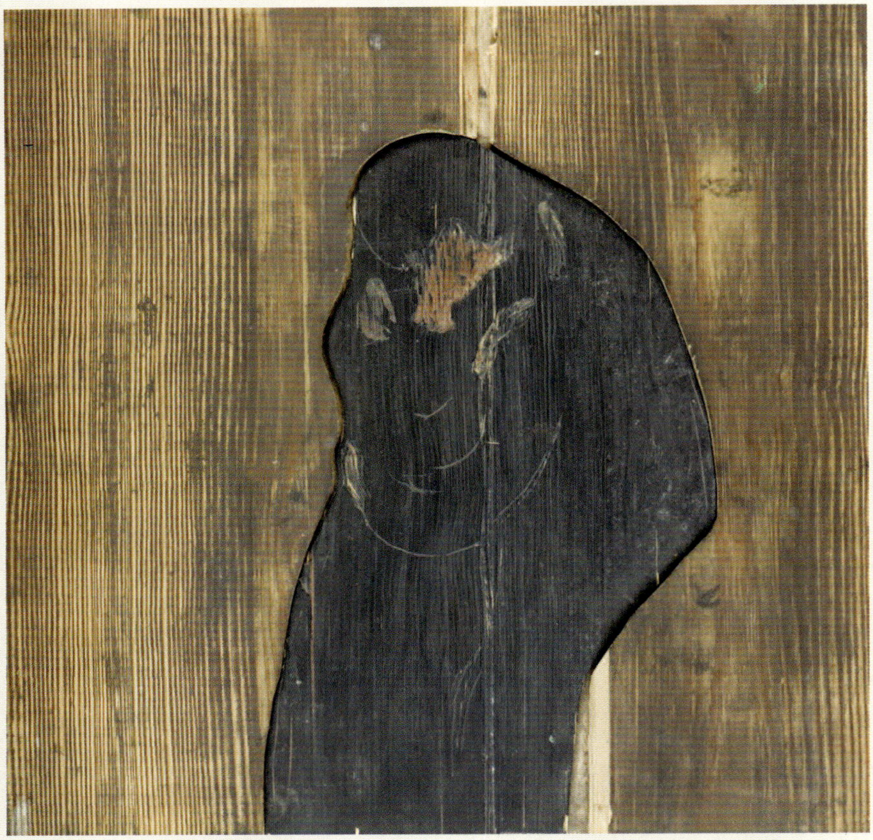

33 *The Kiss IV*, 1902, woodcut

The Kiss is a love subject that appeared among Munch's first prints in 1895. He eventually made four woodcut versions of this beautifully simple subject. Munch presents his lovers poetically as interlocked trees, or as metamorphosing into a single trunk, an idea reinforced by the prominent woodgrain of the colour block. A version of *The Kiss* was exhibited in Paris at the Bing Gallery (1896) and it was described by the misogynist Strindberg as '...the fusion of two beings one of which in the form of a carp, seems to be about to swallow the larger' (Hodin, 1972, 75).

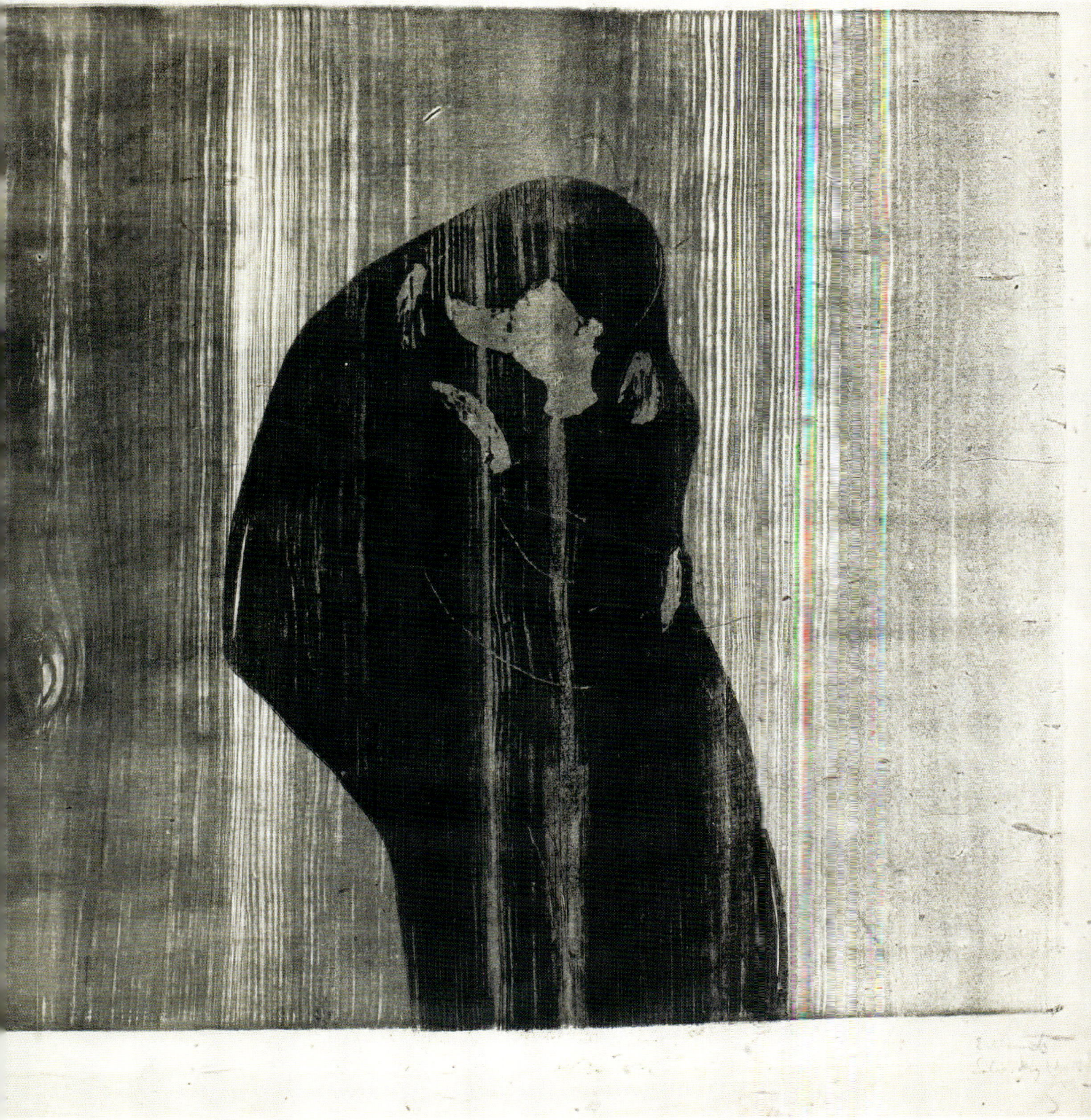

Fig. 16 Bella Edwards and Eva Mudocci, the musicians in *The Violin Concert* (34), B2343 (F)

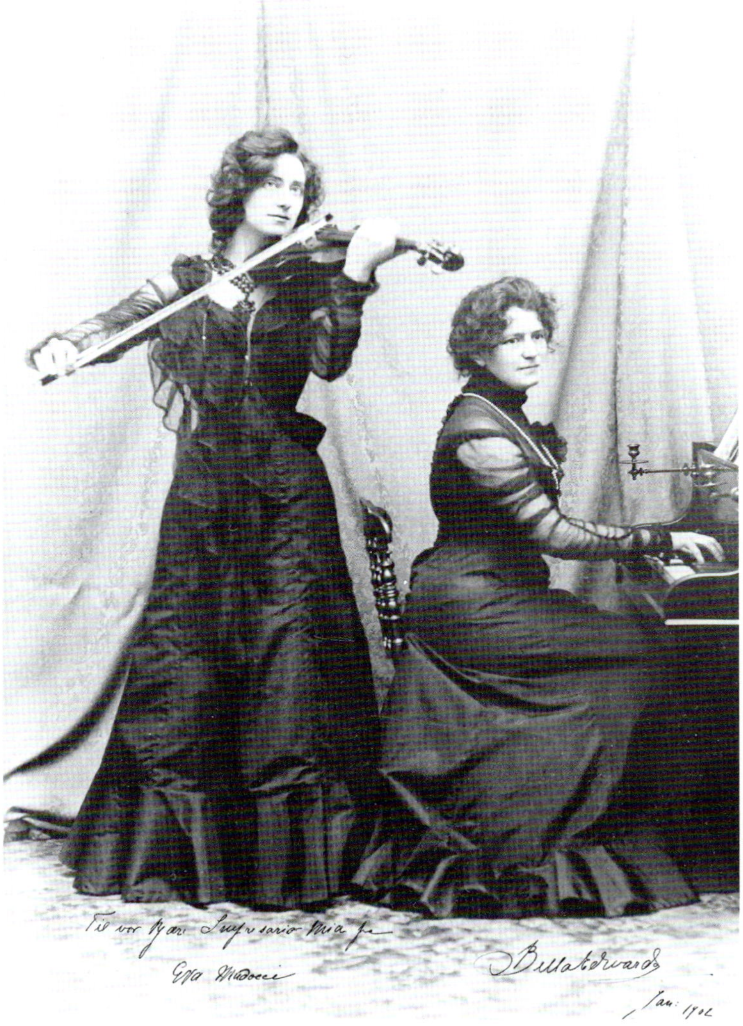

34. *Violin Concert*, 1903, lithograph

The musicians are Bella Edwards (1866–1954) and Evangeline Hope Muddock (1883–1953), who was known by her performing name of Eva Mudocci, and with whom Munch began a relationship in Paris in 1903. Munch also made two lithograph portraits of Mudocci (35 and W.244). Both musicians were well known in Scandinavia and France, where Bella was a friend of Matisse, for whom she sometimes posed as a model.

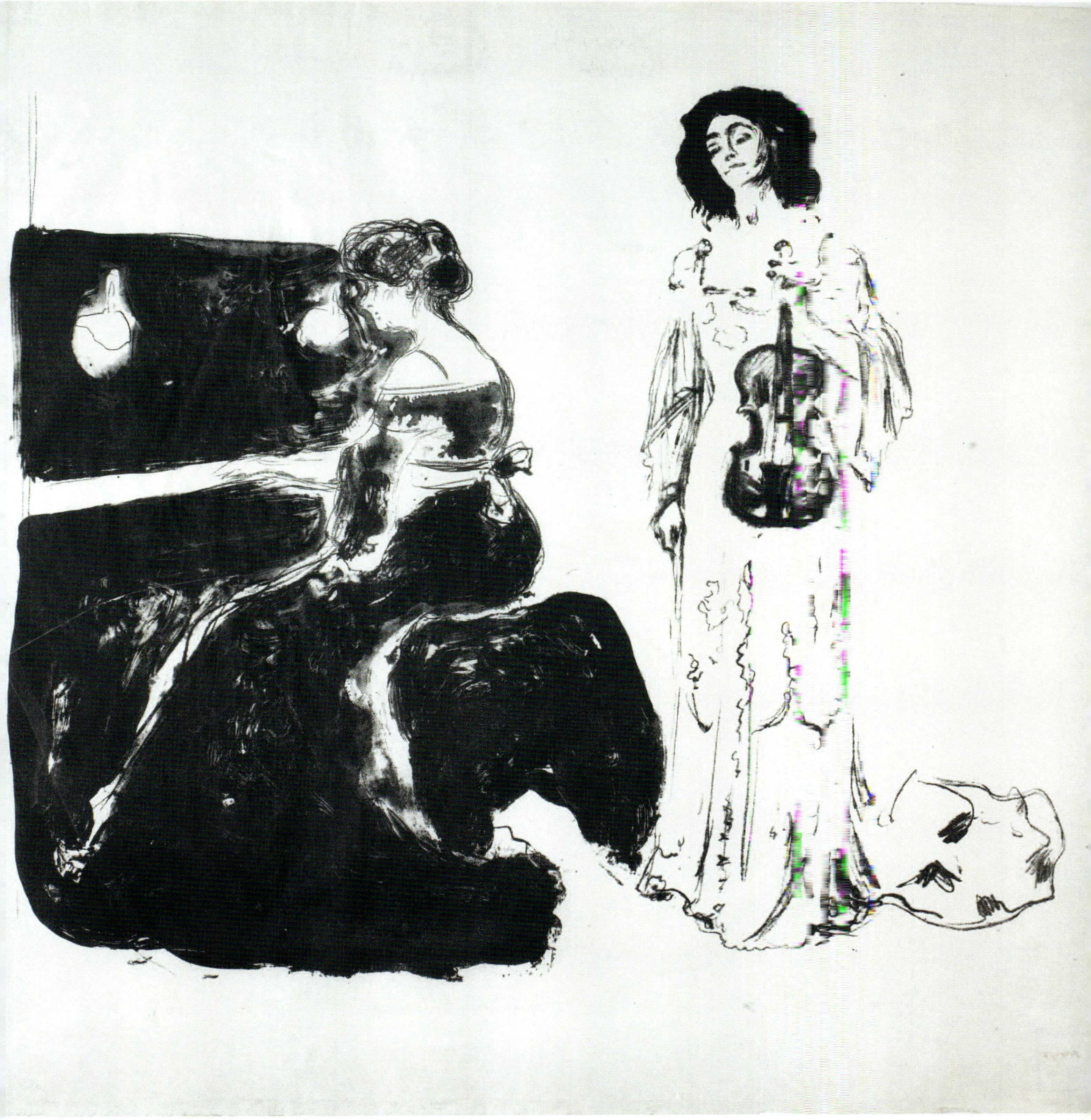

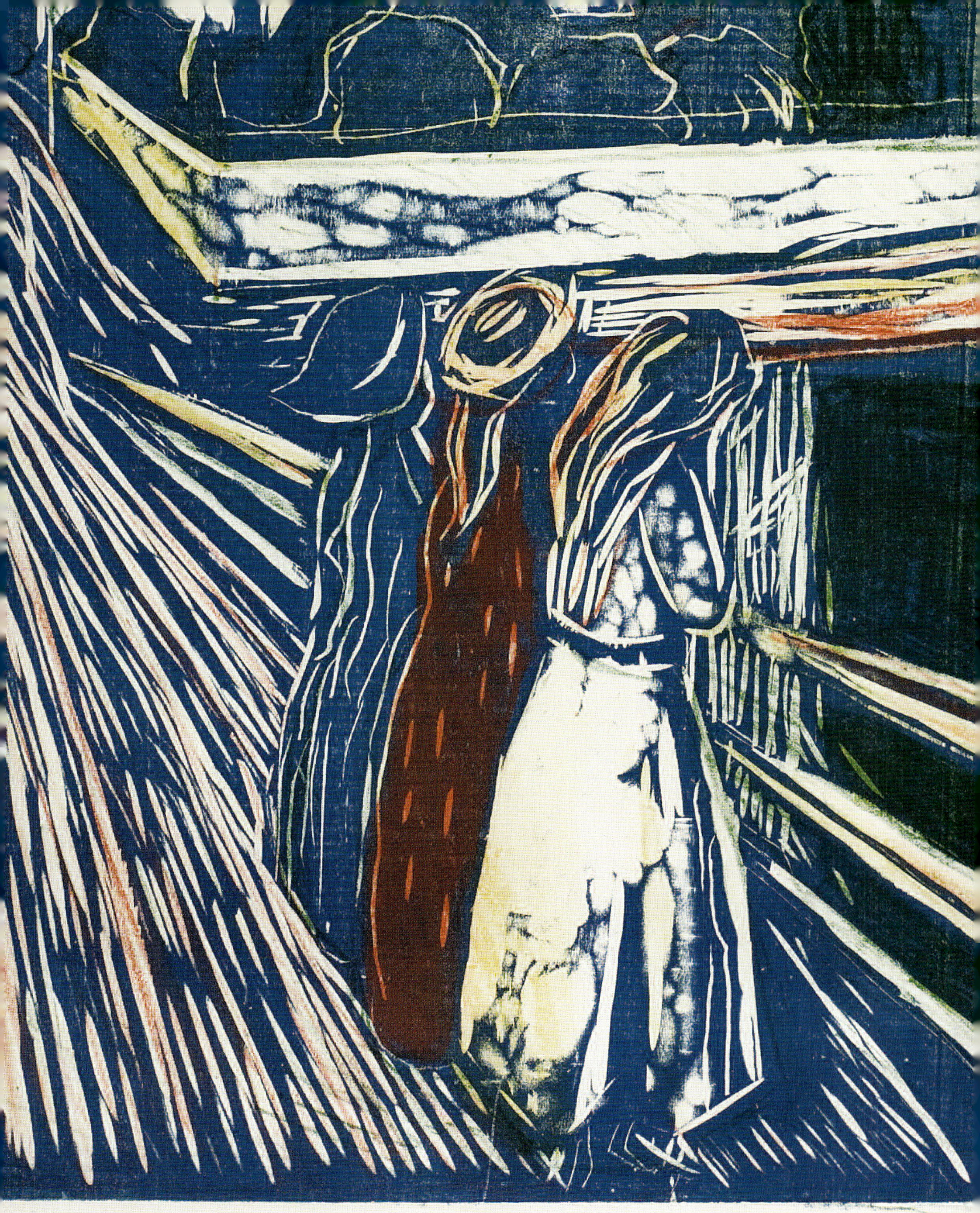

Chronology

1863 Munch born at Løten to a military doctor, Christian Munch, and Laura Bjølstad, who already have one daughter, Johanne Sophie. Further siblings: Peter Andreas born 1865, Laura Catherine 1867 and Inger Marie 1868.

1864 Munch's family moves to Kristiania (later called Oslo).

1867 Death of Charles Baudelaire. Henrik Ibsen, *Peer Gynt*.

1868 Munch's mother dies of tuberculosis soon after Inger's birth.

1871 Unification of Germany. Publication of James McNeill Whistler's *Thames Set* etchings. Charles Darwin, *The Descent of Man*; Friedrich Nietzsche, *The Birth of Tragedy*.

1874 First Impressionist Exhibition in Paris.

1875 Manet makes five lithographs for Edgar Allan Poe's *Raven*, translated by Stéphane Mallarmé.

1876 Stéphane Mallarmé, *The Afternoon of a Faun*, illustrated by Manet.

1877 Death of Munch's older sister Sophie.

1879 Attends Technical College, intending to study engineering but abandons this in 1880 to study art.

1880 Whistler, *12 Etchings of Venice*; Max Klinger, *Eva and the Future*.

1881 Attends Kristiania's Royal School of Art and Design. Ibsen, *Ghosts*.

1882 Rents a studio in Pultosten with fellow artists, including Christian Krohg, Erik Werenskiold and Fritz Thaulow. Krohg organises first independent Autumn Exhibition. Munch publishes book of humorous prints, *Pen Drawings*.

1883 Exhibits first painting: *Study of the Head of a Red-haired*

The Girls on the Bridge (detail), 1918, woodcut and lithograph

35 *Salome*, 1903, lithograph

One of two portraits of the beautiful violinist Eva Mudocci. The other presents her as a Madonna (W.244), emphasising her beautiful hair. This print was made at the same time, and according to the print collector Schiefler, her representation as Salome, with the artist's disembodied head under her arm, was the result of a slip of the hand. Oscar Wilde's 1891 play turned the biblical princess Salome into the 'Goddess of Decadence'. Munch owned Aubrey Beardsley's celebrated illustrations to *Salome* (1894), and the first performance of the play had been staged in Paris shortly before he arrived in 1896.

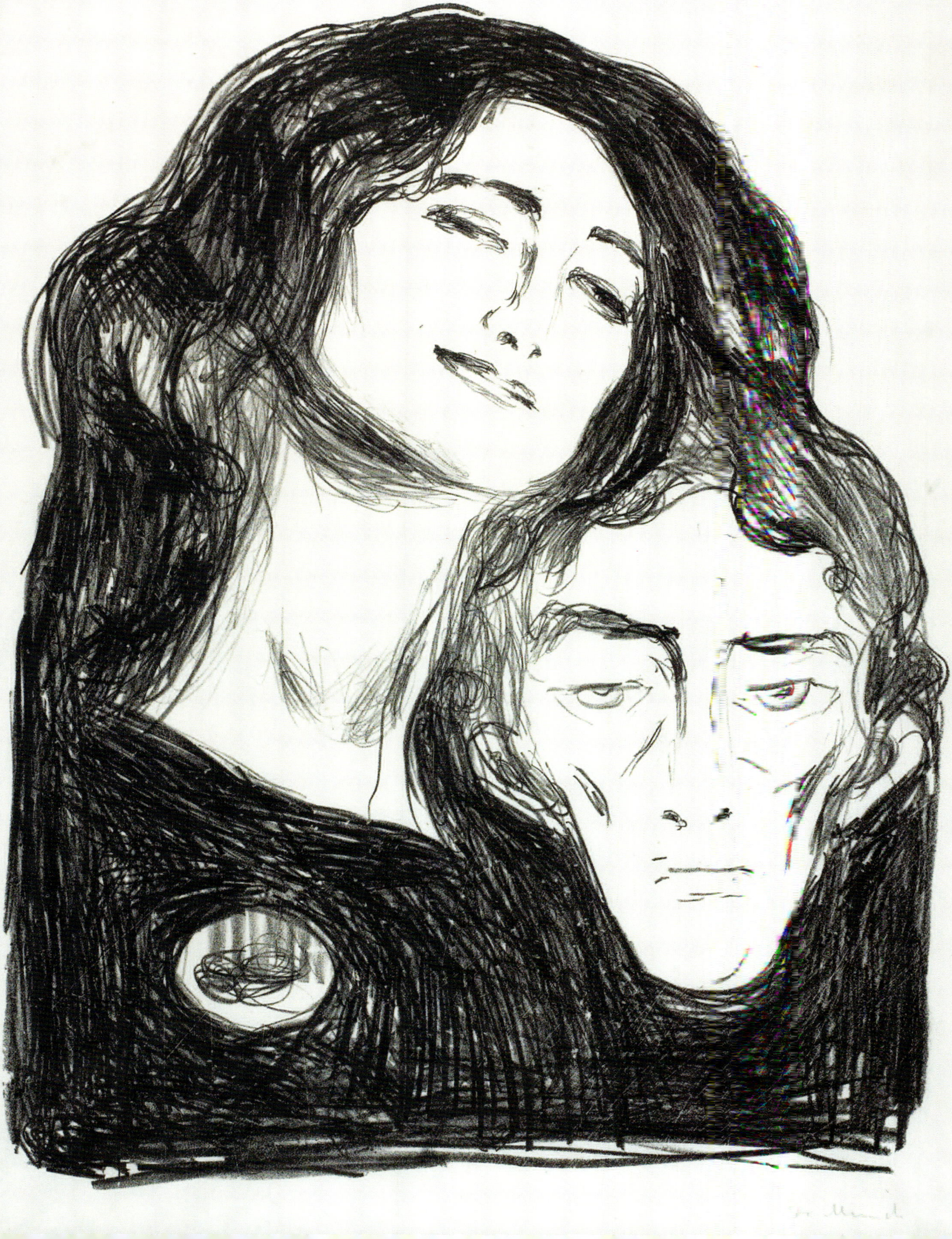

Woman; attends open-air academy of Fritz Thaulow, Modum. Earliest pictures painted in a French-influenced, *plein-air* style.

1884 Participates for the first time in Autumn Exhibition in Kristiania, in which several works by Gauguin are also shown. In contact with the 'Kristiania Bohemians' who meet at the Grand Café.

1885 To Paris via Antwerp for three weeks; impressed by Manet. On return starts work on pivotal paintings, *The Sick Child*, *Puberty* and *The Morning After*. August Strindberg, *Married* Vol II; Hans Jaeger, *From the Kristiania Bohemians*. Begins love affair with Milly Thaulow.

1886 *The Sick Child* exhibited in Kristiania Autumn Exhibition. Paints first version of *Madonna*. Ibsen, *Rosmersholm*.

1887 Six paintings in Autumn Exhibition.

1889–92 Living mostly in Paris.

1889 First one-man show in Kristiania. Rents house in Åsgårdstrand, which he subsequently buys. To Paris October 1889–91, with state scholarship to study, initially with Léon Bonnat; first-hand experience of Impressionism. November: Munch's father dies. Max Klinger, *On Death I*.

1890 Living in St Cloud with Danish poet Emmanuel Goldstein. Summer in Norway at Åsgårdstrand and Kristiania.

1892 Pictures exhibited in Kristiania, rejected by critics; invited to show in Berlin with the Verein Berliner Künstler; angry reception of his pictures; exhibition closes after one week, but is later shown elsewhere. The scandal immediately makes Munch one of the best-known artists in Germany.

1893–1908 Living mostly in Berlin.

1893 Blomqvist Gallery in Kristiania organises its first 'black and white' exhibition: a mixture of reproductive and original prints. In Berlin exhibits fifty pictures, some presented as *A Human Life*, and another series known as *From the Modern Life of the Soul*. Friendships include Stanislaw Przybyszewski, Richard Dehmel, Julius Meier-Graefe, Strindberg, Sigbjørn Obstfelder, Gustav Vigeland, Axel Gallén and Jens Thiis.

1894 First book on Munch, *The Work of Edvard Munch*, published in Berlin by Przybyszewski, Franz Servaes, Willy Pastor and Julius Meier-Graefe. Makes first drypoints and etchings, and first lithograph, *Puberty* (W. 14). *Death and*

36 *Friedrich Nietzsche*, 1906, lithograph

Nietzsche's antireligious works, such as *Human, All Too Human* (1878) and *Thus Spake Zarathustra* (1883), were enormously influential on Munch's generation. In Weimar, Munch met the great philosopher's sister, and painted a related portrait for his Swedish patron, the banker Ernest Thiel. Munch wrote that the image of the sun behind the philosopher was a reference to *Thus Spake Zarathustra*, alluding '...to the passage where he speaks about standing in the light but wishing he were in the dark' (Lathe, 1979, 23). This print was made at the Weimarer Kunstschule. Only four impressions are known.

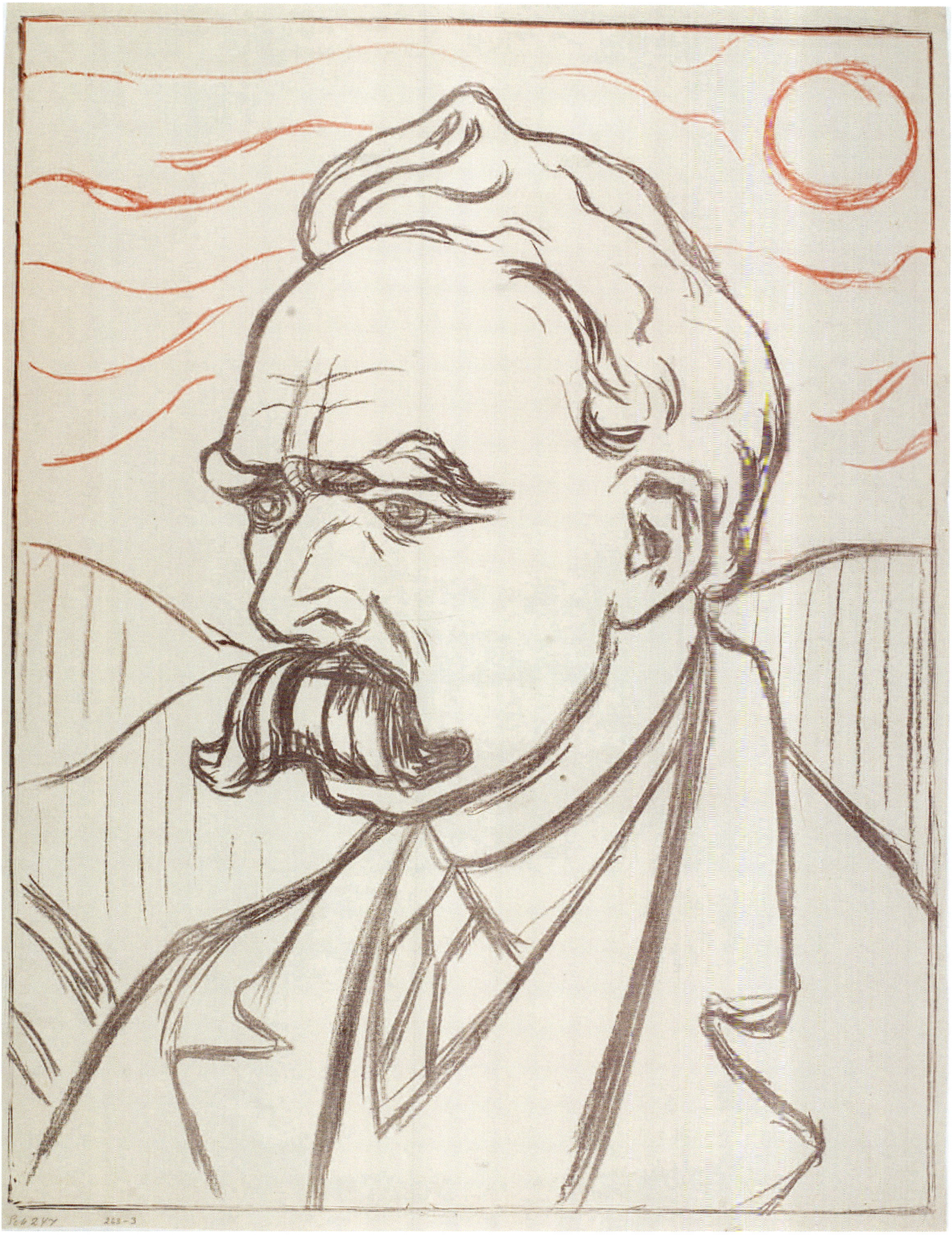

the Woman (1), *The Day After* (2), *Madonna* (3), *Summer Night. The Voice* (4).

1895 To Paris, twice. March: exhibition at Ugo Barroccio Gallery, Berlin includes seventeen prints and drawings. Ibsen visits Munch's exhibition in Kristiania, which is reviewed in *Revue Blanche.* May: Count Harry Kessler introduces Munch to Joseph Sattler so that he can learn transfer lithography, permitting drawing on paper rather than on stone. *The Scream* (9) reproduced in December issue of *Revue Blanche.* Julius Meier-Graefe publishes portfolio of eight intaglio prints by Munch: the prints are advertised in *Pan.* Recognition by Paris intelligentsia. Death of brother Andreas. *Kristiania Bohemians II* (5), *Moonlight. Night in St Cloud* (6), *Woman II* (7), *Self-Portrait* (8), *The Scream, Madonna* (10), *Vampire II* (11), *Stanislaw Przybyszewski* (12).

1896 Year of important printmaking activity: Munch makes forty-nine prints, including twenty-five lithographs and his first woodcuts. In Paris, working on lithographs and first woodcuts at Atelier Clot. Makes lithograph *Angst* for Vollard's *Album of Painter-printmakers* portfolio. First performance of Oscar Wilde's *Salomé.* Meets Mallarmé; May: exhibition at Bing's Salon de l'Art Nouveau, includes forty-one prints. Commission to illustrate Baudelaire's *The Flowers of Evil* (not completed). June: Strindberg writes about Munch in *Revue Blanche.* Summer: paints in Norway at Åsgårdstrand. Paintings exhibited at Salon des Indépendants include *Madonna, Vampire* and *The Scream.* November: Munch makes lithograph playbill for Ibsen's *Peer Gynt,* Théâtre de l'Oeuvre. Makes first woodcuts. *Death in the Sickroom* (13), *August Strindberg* (14), *Jealousy I* (15), *The Sick Child I* (16), *Attraction I* (17), *Separation II* (18), *On the Waves of Love* (19), *Moonlight I* (20), *Evening. Melancholy I* (21), *Angst* (22).

1897 March: visits Brussels, where seven prints are included in exhibition of La Libre Esthétique. Exhibits pictures from the *Frieze of Life* at Salon des Indépendants, Paris. October: sixty-four prints exhibited at Kristiania Diorama, including a series of eighteen lithographs and four woodcuts presented as a portfolio entitled *The Mirror.* Prints included were *On the Waves of Love, Madonna, Attraction I, Jealousy, Vampire, The Scream, Evening. Melancholy I* and *Angst.*

37 *Young Women on the Beach II,* 1907, drypoint

In 1907 Gustav Schiefler published the first volume of his *Catalogue of Edvard Munch's Graphic Works to 1906.* Intaglio prints had been Schiefler's first love, and he encouraged Munch to make woodcut decorations and supply original prints for inclusion in the publication. This landscape subject of girls on the shore at Åsgårdstrand is similar to the drypoint *From Åsgårdstrand* (W. 289), which was included in the book to give an impression of a place that was dear to the artist.

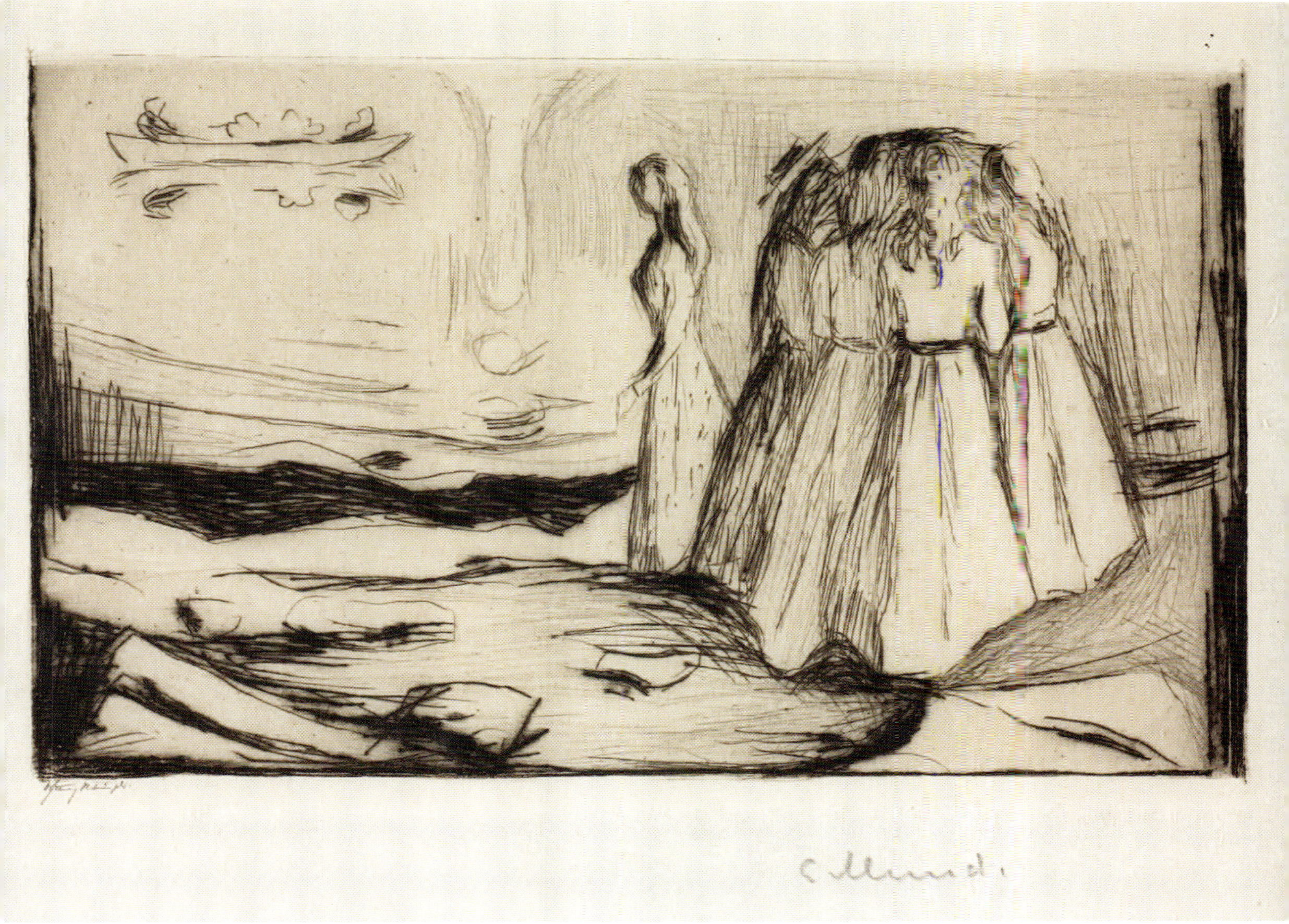

38 *Moonlight by the Sea*, 1912, woodcut

Munch's obsession with the figures of man or woman on the Åsgårdstrand shore emerges from several important prints of the years 1896–1902. This later version of woman contains the same essential elements (7, 18, 26). Munch's male figure is characteristically humble before the vastness of the sea, but the young woman looks out more confidently: she has very long (usually blood-red) hair, which represents part of her fascination for the artist. Munch's motif of the column of moonlight (or sunlight) provides a symbolic pathway, always incomplete, between land and sky.

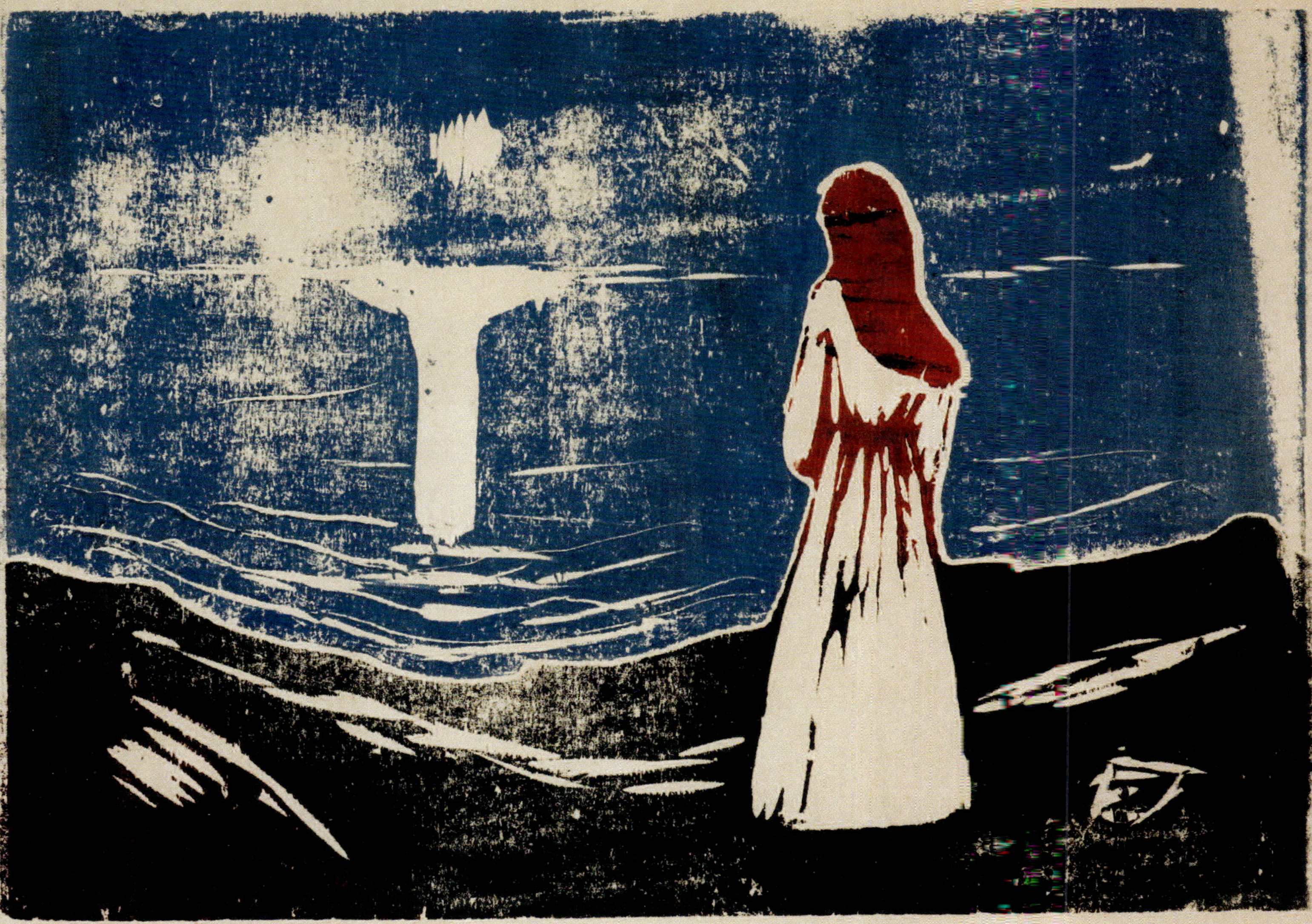

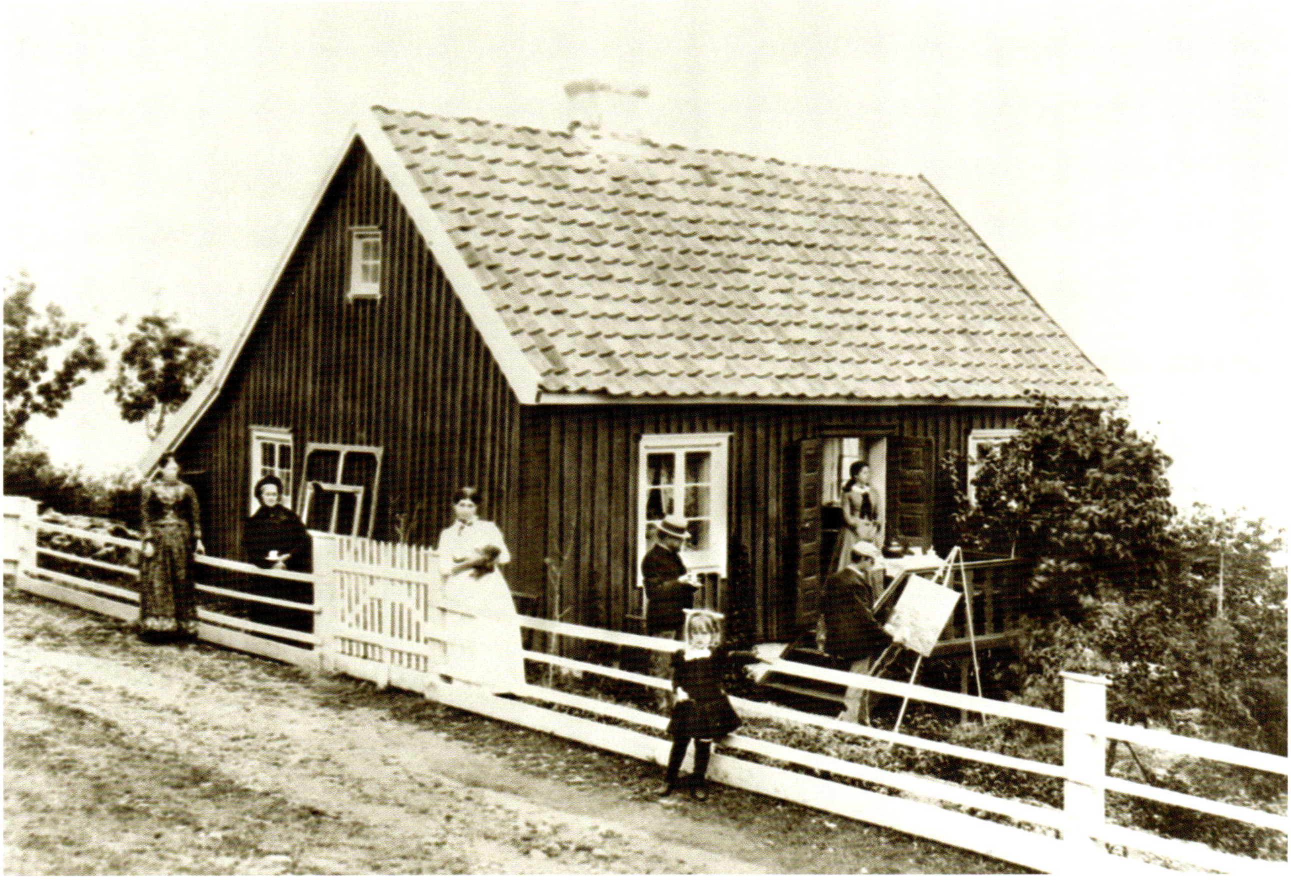

Fig. 17 The Munch family at Åsgårdstrand, 1889, with Edvard at his easel

Letter from Munch to Julius Meier-Graefe states that woodcuts were being printed with colour added from lithographic stones. Summer: goes to Åsgårdstrand. *Stéphane Mallarmé* (23), *In the Man's Brain* (24).

1898 Two paintings and thirty-one prints bought by National Gallery, Kristiania (director: Jens Thiis). Installs small press for printing woodcuts and lithographs. Meets Mathilde (Tulla) Larsen. Travels with Larsen in the spring to Italy. *Melancholy II* (25), *Two Women on the Shore* (26).

1899 To Florence and Rome via Berlin. Autumn and winter in sanatorium in Gudbrandsdalen. Prints lithographs in Kristiania with Petersen & Weitz. Prints woodcuts himself. *Woman's Head against the Shore* (28), *Two Human Beings. The Lonely Ones* (29)

1900 May: exhibits paintings and two woodcuts in Dresden.

1901 Summer in Åsgårdstrand. Settles in Berlin again in November. September: exhibition in Kristiania includes thirty-four prints. Transports plates, lithographic stones and woodblocks from Norway to Berlin for printing.

1902 Prolific year for printmaking, especially etching. Makes new versions of woodblocks of 1896. Stays in Lübeck with Dr Max Linde, for whom he makes portfolio of fourteen etchings and two lithographs. To Weimar, staying with Count Harry Kessler. Summer in Norway. Dramatic end to the relationship with Tulla Larsen, who threatens to kill herself; Munch's hand is wounded in the struggle. The separation leads to a break with friends sympathetic to Tulla. Critical breakthrough at the Berlin Sezession, showing twenty-two pictures forming a series later titled the *Frieze of Life*. Three prints included in Vienna Sezession. Exhibitions of prints in Bergen and Dresden. *Woman with Red Hair and Green Eyes. The Sin* (30), *Henrik Ibsen at the Grand Café* (31), *Melancholy III* (32) and *The Kiss IV* (33).

1903 Summer in Åsgårdstrand, autumn in Berlin and Lübeck. Meets English violinist Eva Mudocci in Paris. Good sales of prints. Exhibits paintings and prints with Bruno Cassirer, Berlin, who proposes to sell prints outside Scandinavia. Twenty-two prints included in Munich Sezession; forty-seven prints in Berlin Sezession. Also exhibits prints in Hamburg, Leipzig and Warsaw. First meeting with print collector Gustav Schiefler in Hamburg. First prints acquired by Friedrich Lippmann for Berlin Kupferstichkabinett. *The Violin Concert* (34), *Salome* (35).

1904 Exhibits ninety works, including prints at National Gallery, Kristiania. Spring: lithographic stones sent by Lemercier, Paris, to Lassally in Berlin. Contract with Bruno Cassirer gives exclusive right to sell prints in Germany for three years. Gustav Schiefler begins first complete catalogue of Munch's prints.

1905 Norway and Sweden separate. January: exhibits sixty-three prints in Copenhagen; February: forty-six prints in Prague; November: exhibits 149 prints at R. Piper & Co., Munich.

1906 In Berlin, designs sets for Max Reinhardt's productions of Ibsen's *Ghosts* and *Hedda Gabler*. Paints *Self-portrait with Bottle of Wine*. February: exhibits twenty paintings at Sächsischer Kunstverein, Dresden. Invited by Karl Schmidt-Rottluff to contribute woodcuts to the first exhibition of Die Brücke in Dresden. *Friedrich Nietzsche* (36).

1907 Spends summer at German resort of Warnemünde. Cassirer publishes Schiefler's catalogue of the prints, which

39 *Young Couple in a Spruce Forest*, 1915, woodcut

World War I was a period during which the Norwegian economy became stronger as a result of political neutrality, and Munch was stimulated to make new prints as well as reprint old plates, blocks and stones. This print of lovers in the woods by the sea at Åsgårdstrand (4, 27) is one of fifteen new woodcut subjects made in the years 1915–16. By this time, Munch had long abandoned the idea that he himself might find a woman to be his life partner. However, the same images that he had worked on as a young man before his disillusionment and mental collapse in 1908 still obsessed him.

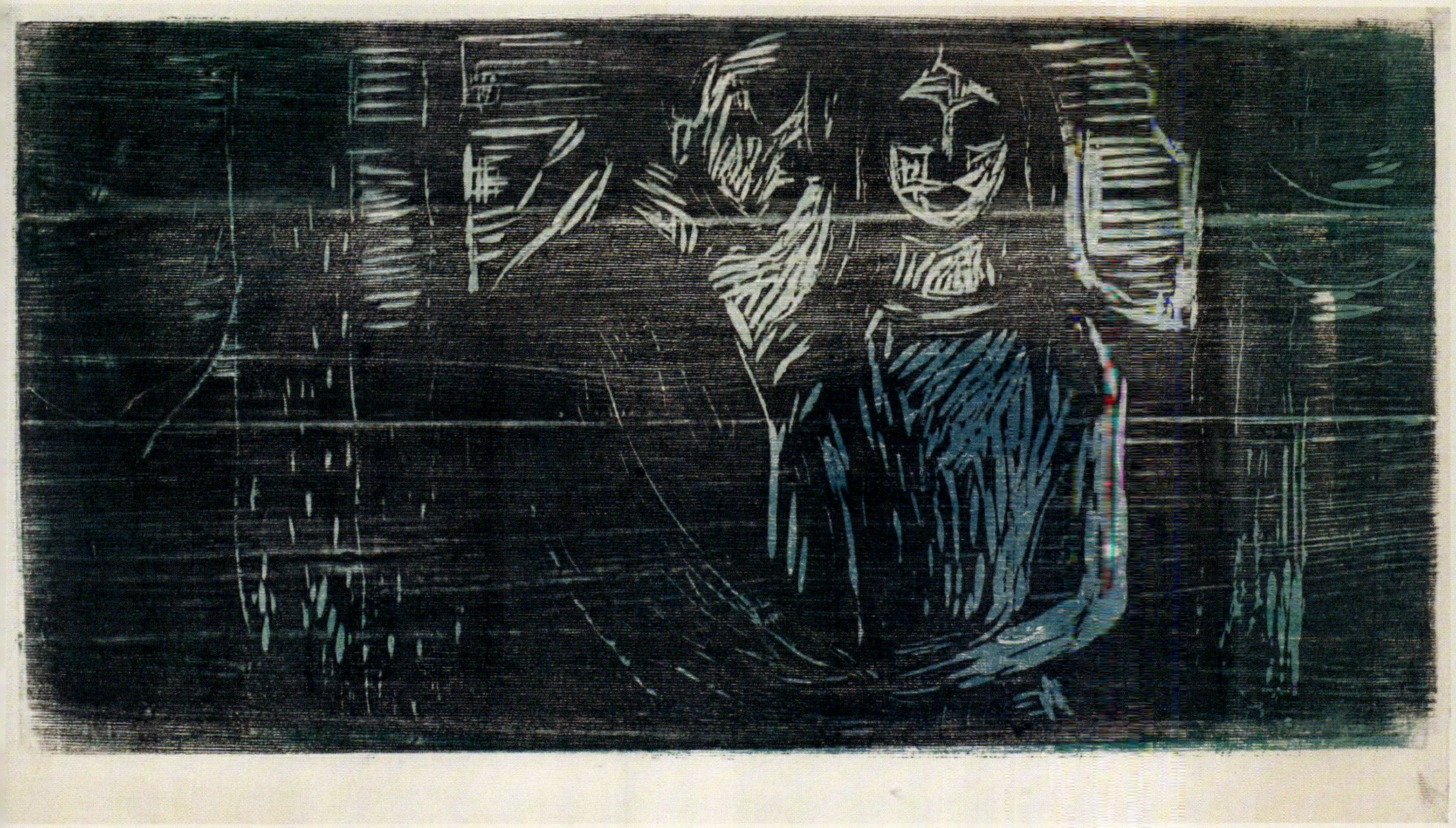

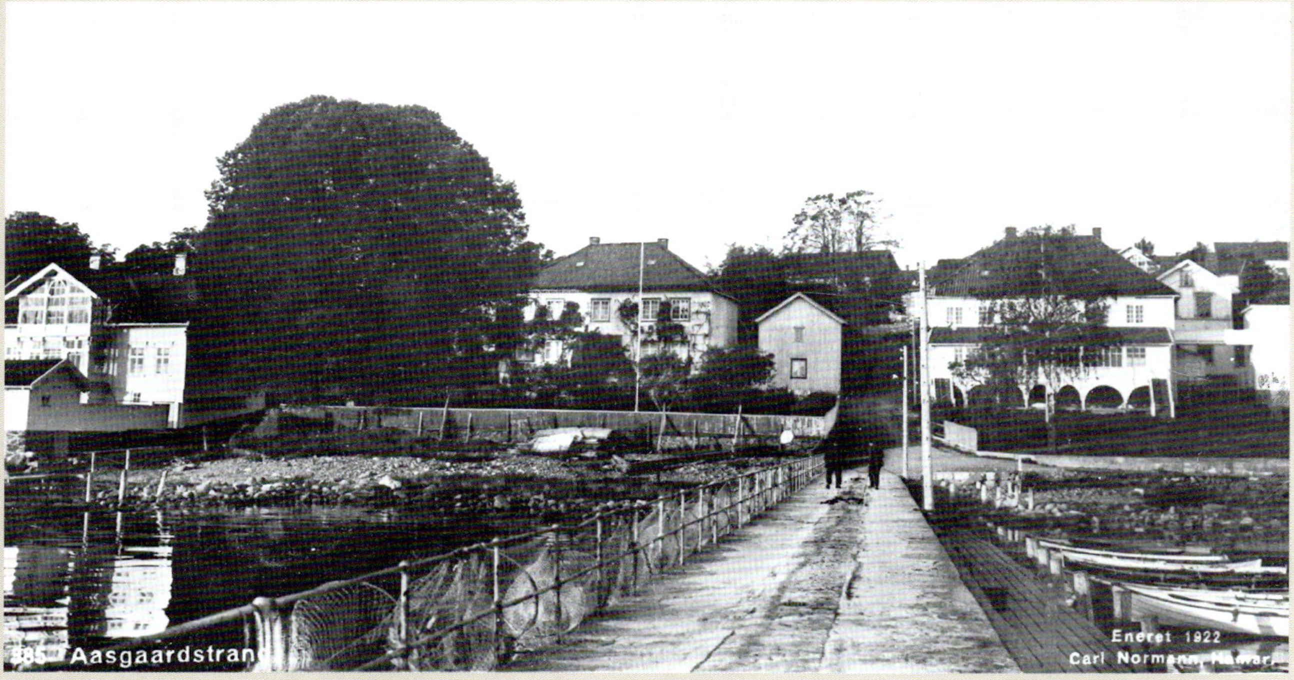

Fig. 18 The pier at Åsgårdstrand, photo by Carl Normann Hamar, B1796 (F)

40 *The Girls on the Bridge*, 1918, woodcut and lithograph

The pier at Åsgårdstrand appears in many of Munch's works. Åsgårdstrand is the village where, from 1889, Munch rented and later owned a small house in which he spent his summers. The shore with its landing stage, the Kjøsterud House and the distinctive lime tree next to it provides the setting for a number of Munch's most dramatic images (17, 21, 25, 32). The pier was the arrival point for visitors from Kristiania, who would travel there by boat at weekends. The implication of the image is that the women are waiting for their lovers to arrive on the next boat.

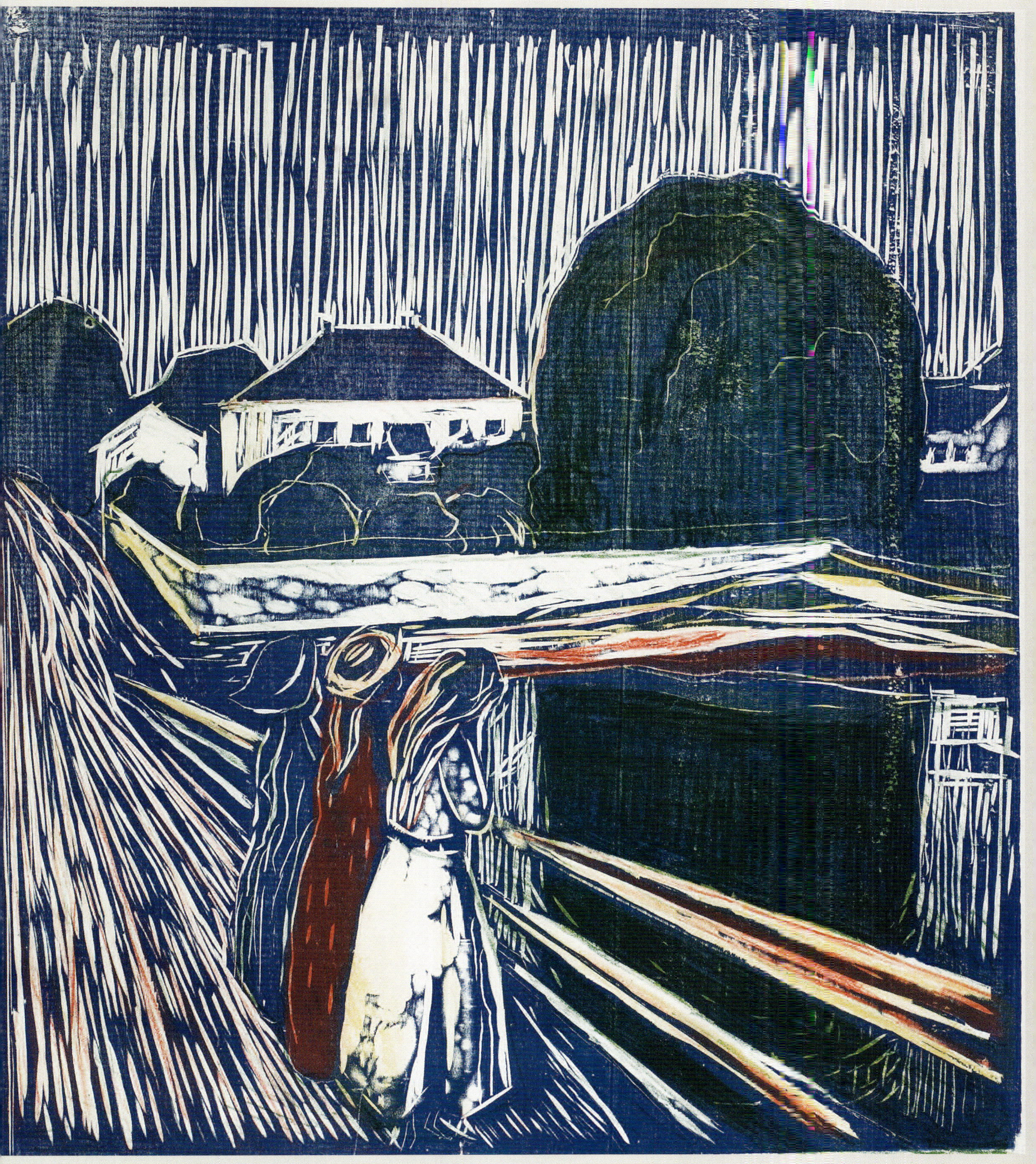

establishes Munch as a major figure. Exhibits twenty-four prints at Berlin Sezession. *Young Women on the Beach II* (37).

1908 Suffers nervous breakdown; treated in Dr Jacobsen's clinic for eight months. Writes prose poem *Alpha and Omega*, accompanied by lithographs. Large purchase of paintings by National Gallery, Kristiania. Exhibits sixty-five prints at Kunstforeningen, Copenhagen; twenty-six prints at Berlin Sezession; about eighty prints at Kunstsalon Bock, Hamburg. Also exhibits prints in Mannheim, Bremen and Munich.

1909 Begins work on mural paintings for the Aula of Kristiania University (completed in 1914). January: exhibits ninety-nine prints in Helsinki; March: two hundred prints and drawings in Kristiania, touring to Bergen, Stavanger and Kristiansand. Exhibits prints from *Alpha And Omega* series at Berlin Sezession.

1910 Major exhibition in Kristiania includes c.180 prints. Buys estate at Hvitsten on Kristiania fjord. Probable meeting with lithographic printer Anton Peder Nielsen of the firm Halvorsen & Larsen in Kristiania.

1911 Purchases lithographic press. Orders reprints of all stones in Berlin. Exhibits 141 prints at Kristiania Diorama. Wins competition to paint murals for Aula of Kristiania University.

1912 Retrospective exhibition included in the Sonderbund's international exhibition, *New Painting*, Cologne. Munch's section contains thirty-two paintings, more than any artist beside Van Gogh, and comparable to the sections dedicated to Gauguin and Cézanne. Installs lithographic press at Hvitsen. January: exhibits fifty prints with Künstlerbund Hagen, Vienna; August: exhibits eighty prints with J.B. Neumann, Berlin; October: exhibits with Gurlitt; November: exhibits twelve prints in Berlin Sezession; recently acquired prints exhibited at Kupferstichkabinett, Berlin. First contact between Munch and Curt Glaser at the Kupferstichkabinett. *Moonlight by the Sea* (38).

1913 Major print shows in Breslau, Berlin, Dresden, Düsseldorf and Hamburg; exhibits eight prints at New York Armory show. Installs new intaglio press.

1914 Start of World War I. Norway celebrates a hundred years of independence. Requests return from Berlin of all metal plates and woodblocks. Lithographic stones remain as property of Lassally. Makes intaglio prints in Paris. February:

exhibits thirty prints at Kestner-Museum, Hannover; March: 109 prints at Amsler & Ruthardt, Berlin.

1915 Concentrates on printmaking: using transfer paper, reworks lithographs, originally made in Berlin, on new stones; makes new proofs of most metal plates and woodblocks in his possession. Exhibits 221 prints at Bergen Kunstforeningen; fifty-seven prints included in Norwegian section, Panama-Pacific International Exposition, San Francisco. Also exhibits prints at Kunstnerforbundet, Kristiania and Kupferstichkabinett, Berlin. *Young Couple in a Spruce Forest* (39).

1916 Purchases estate of Ekely at Skøyen where he lives for rest of life. Reprints large number of intaglio prints and lithographs. Regular visits from Nielsen of Halvorsen & Larsen to print lithographs and woodcuts. Unveiling of Aula murals, Kristiania University.

1917 Curt Glaser publishes *Edvard Munch*. Exhibits c.400 prints at Blomqvist's Gallery, Kristiania, and distributes catalogue of his work known as the Nordic catalogue.

1918 Exhibits prints in Trondheim, Dresden, Bremen, Hamburg and Stockholm. *The Girls on the Bridge* (40).

1919 Builds studio at Ekely. Exhibits fifty-seven prints at Bourgeois Galleries, New York. Society for Norwegian Printmakers (Norske Grafikere) is founded in Kristiania.

1920 Berlin dealer J.B. Neumann organises exhibition Munch und die Künstler der Brücke at Bremen Kunsthalle.

1922 Major exhibition at Kunsthaus, Zurich, including 433 prints. Through Curt Glaser, Munch purchases prints from German artists suffering in the depression.

1924 Exhibits prints in Vienna, Prague, Hamburg and Berlin. Gives prints to benefit German artists.

1925 Kristiania is renamed Oslo.

1926 Thielska Galleriet, Stockholm, containing the Thiel collection of Munch's work, opens to public. 148 prints exhibited at Kunsthalle, Mannheim.

1927 Important retrospective exhibition in Berlin and Oslo; Oslo show includes a hundred prints from National Gallery; in Berlin the Kupferstichkabinett shows 150 prints.

1928 Exhibits eighty-nine prints at Graphisches Kabinett, Munich. Publication of second volume of Schiefler's catalogue raisonné.

41 *Self-portrait with Bottle of Wine*, 1930, lithograph

Munch's many self-portraits include two impressive lithographs. In the first (8), Munch powerfully proclaims his artistic strength as a white apparition against a pure black background. This late work is based nostalgically on a painting done in Weimar in 1906, towards the end of the artist's most creative phase. It is an image of alienation and despair, painted shortly before his complete nervous breakdown. Writing in December 1929, Munch looked back on this time, remembering '...the days before I was admitted to the Clinic in Copenhagen, the way I senselessly poured wine and Cognac down my throat and smoked the strongest cigars.'

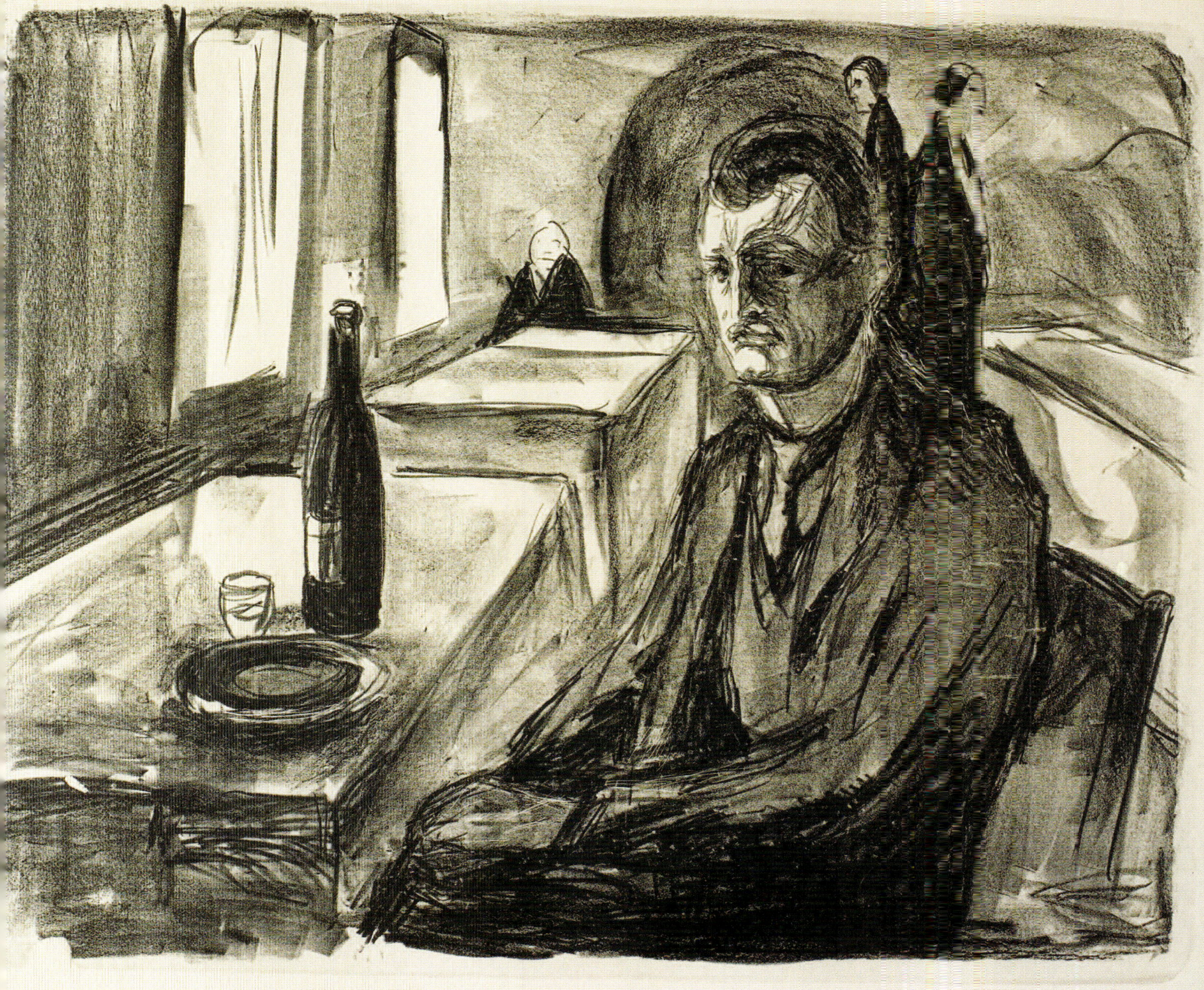

1929 246 prints exhibited at Stockholm, Nationalmuseum; exhibits 107 prints at Leipzig; prints also exhibited at Dresden, Oslo, Berlin, Kiel, Breslau and Chemnitz.

1930 Sets up printmaking workshop in cellar of new studio at Ekely. Draws lithographs directly on stone. Exhibits 197 prints at Galerie Commeter, Hamburg. *Self-portrait with Bottle of Wine* (41).

1931 Fifteen paintings exhibited at the Society of Scottish Artists, Edinburgh; ninety-five prints at Detroit Institute of Arts; ninety-five prints in Bielefeld; ninety-nine prints at Bern Kunsthalle.

1932 Seventy-five prints exhibited at Zürich Kunsthaus.

1936 Four paintings and a number of prints exhibited at The London Gallery. Munch presents two prints to the British Museum.

1937 310 prints exhibited at Swedish Art Club, Stockholm; ninety-six prints exhibited at Stedelijk Museum, Amsterdam.

1938 333 prints auctioned in Oslo.

1939 Auction in Oslo of fifty-seven prints returned from Germany, many of which are acquired by National Gallery.

1940 German occupation of Norway. Munch bequeaths his collection to the city of Oslo.

1942 Thirty-four prints exhibited at Brooklyn Museum. Auction of thirty-nine prints from collection of Jens Thiis, Oslo.

1943 Makes final print, *Hans Jaeger III* (W. 748).

1944 23 January, Munch dies at Ekely.

1950–5 Arts Council travelling exhibition Edvard Munch: Etchings, Woodcuts and Lithographs (catalogue essay by J.P. Hodin) shown at Brighton, Edinburgh and Glasgow; Tate Gallery show includes sixty-three paintings and a hundred prints.

1963 Munch Museum opens in Oslo to house the artist's collection bequeathed to the city: it houses 1,100 paintings, 4,500 drawings and 18,000 prints.

1972 Prints from Epstein collection exhibited at Oberlin, Allen Memorial Art Museum. Travelling exhibition Edvard Munch: The Graphic Work tours UK, beginning in Liverpool and Glasgow.

1973 The Prints of Edvard Munch, Museum of Modern Art, New York; Edvard Munch 1863–1944, Haus der Kunst, Munich, travelling to Paris and London.

1976 Edvard Munch: The Major Graphics, Smithsonian Institution,

Washington D.C.; Edvard Munch, Houston, The Sarah Campbell Blaffer Gallery.

1978 Edvard Munch: Symbols & Images, National Gallery of Art, Washington D.C.

1990 Edvard Munch: Prints, the Charles & Evelyn Kramer Collection at the Tel Aviv Museum of Art; Edvard Munch: Master Prints from the Epstein Family Collection, National Gallery of Art, Washington D.C..

1991 Munch et la France, Musée d'Orsay, Paris.

1997 The Symbolist Prints of Edvard Munch, The Vivian and David Campbell Collection, Toronto, Art Gallery of Ontario.

2001 Edvard Munch: Prints: The Complete Graphic Works, the most comprehensive show of Munch's prints. Gerd Woll, *Edvard Munch: The Complete Graphic Works.*

2003 Edvard Munch: Die Graphik im Berliner Kupferstichkabinett, the most important collection of Munch's graphic work outside Norway.

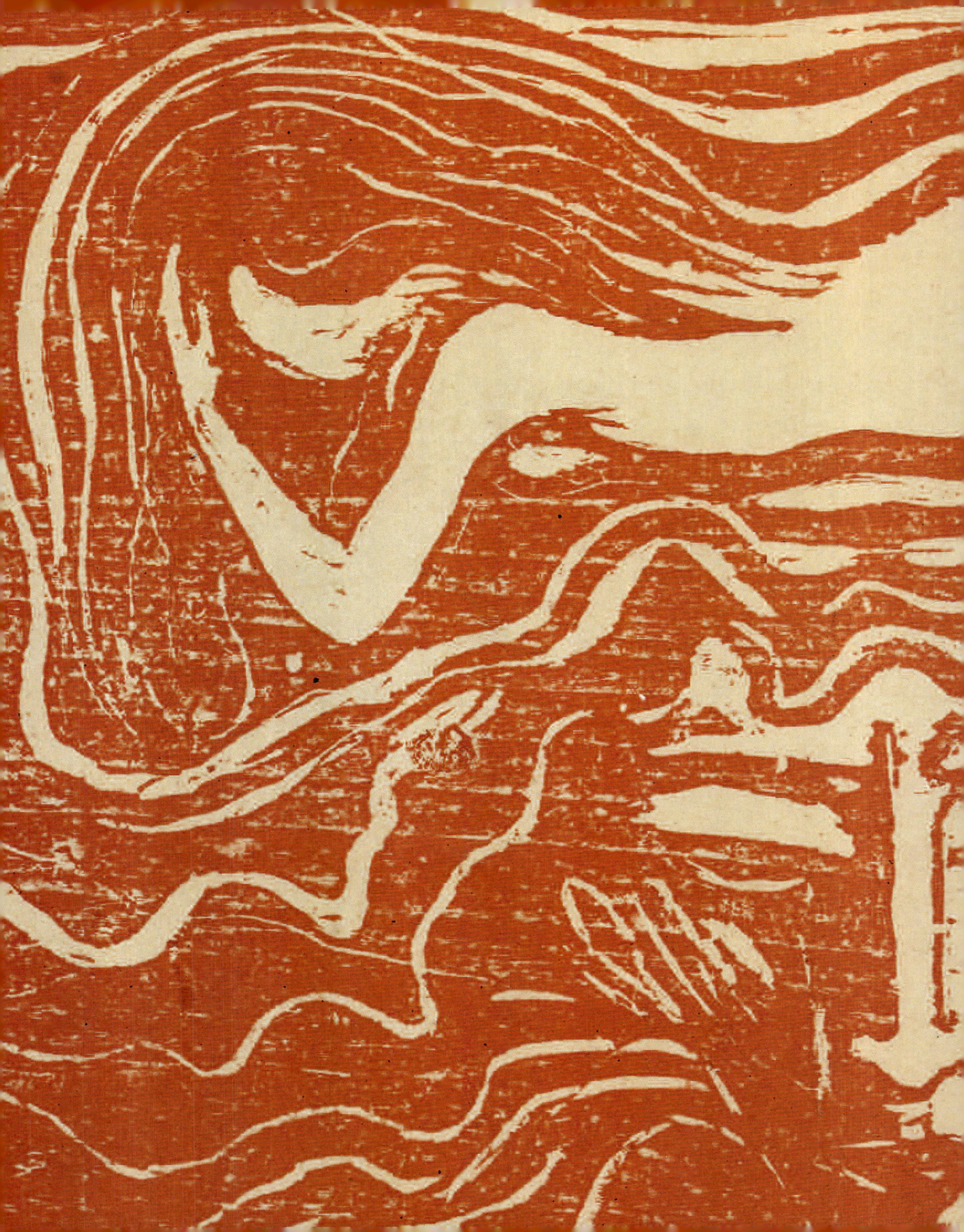

with ink, which remains only on the areas with the drawing.

COLOUR LITHOGRAPH

Normally, a colour lithograph is printed using one stone for each colour of ink. It is possible to print a stone in more than one colour by careful inking.

WOODCUT

Woodcut is a relief printing technique. Munch cut his images into blocks of soft wood using knives and gouges. The areas left in relief print in whatever colour the artist then inks them. Colour woodcuts are most commonly made by separating the image onto a series of blocks, one for each colour. Munch devised a method of cutting up his blocks with a jigsaw so that separate areas could be inked using different colours and the block reassembled for printing. This has become known as the 'puzzle' method. Sometimes Munch used both sides of his blocks for printing the same image, with one face providing the key block and the other being used to print broad areas of colour.

EDITIONS AND HAND COLOURING

Since the middle of the nineteenth century, prints have been sold in limited editions, an artificial device invented to maintain rarity and price. From about 1880, artists began to sign their prints and number them. Although Munch usually signed his prints, he did not number them. Impressions were sometimes taken some years after an image was originally made. Munch also frequently hand coloured impressions of lithographs and woodcuts.

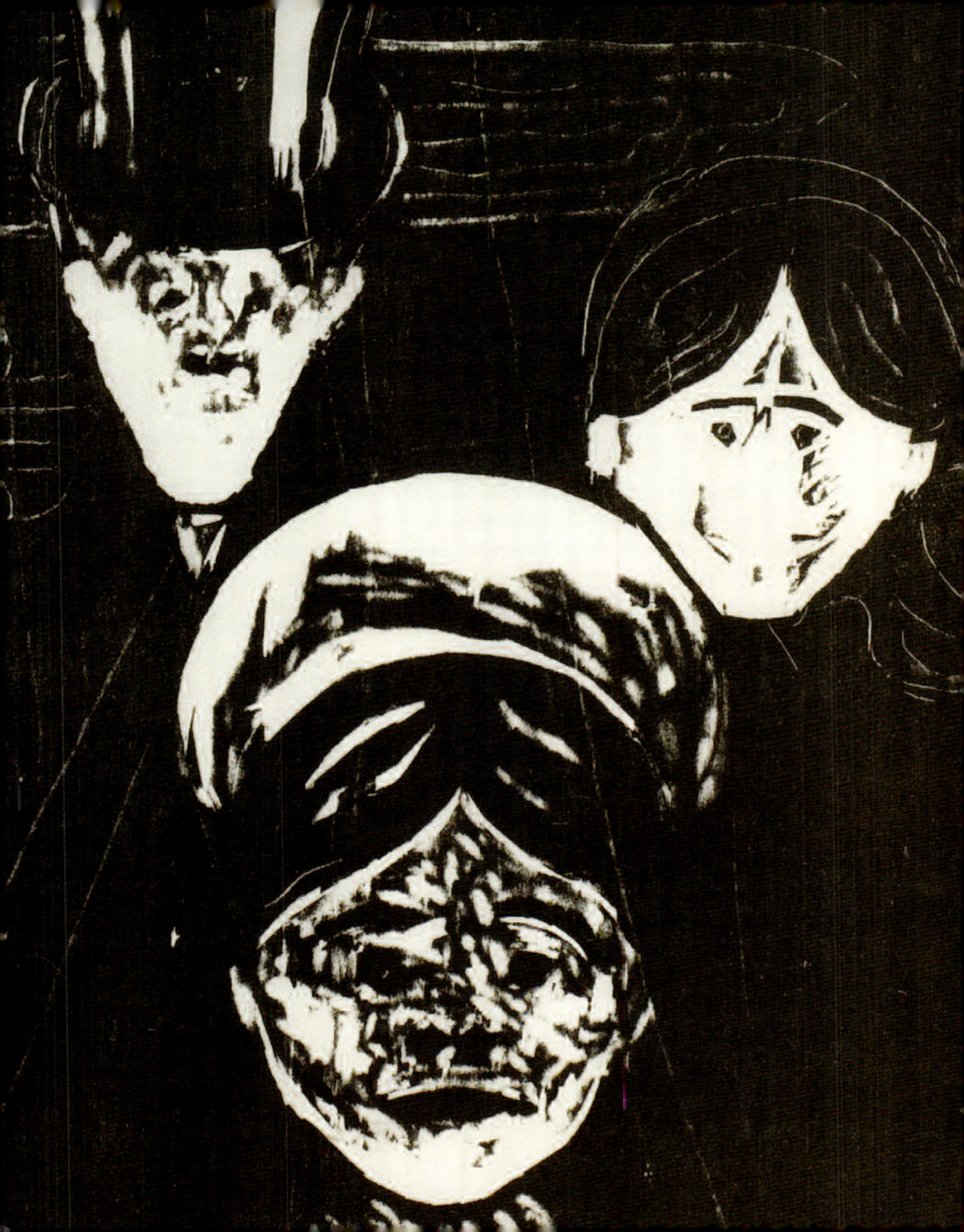

Catalogue

1 *Death and the Woman* 1894
drypoint
23.2 x 16.7
printed by Otto Felsing on wove paper
Munch Museum no. MM G 3–22; W. 3

2 *The Day After* 1894
drypoint
19.1 x 27.3
signed in pencil 'E Munch'
MM G 14–34; W. 10

3 *Madonna* 1894
drypoint
37.9 x 27.9
MM G 15–5. W. 11

4 *Summer Night. The Voice* 1894
etching, open bite and drypoint
23.5 x 31.4
printed by Felsing on wove paper
MM G 18–28; W. 12

5 *Kristiania Bohemians II* 1895
etching, open bite and drypoint
29.8 x 39.8
printed by Felsing on wove paper, signed in pencil
MM G 10–3; W. 16

6 *Moonlight. Night in St Cloud* 1895
drypoint
36.0 x 27.0
printed by Felsing on wove paper
MM G 12–8; W. 17

7 *Woman II (The Woman in three Stages)* 1895
drypoint, etching and open bite
29.0 x 33.0
printed by Felsing on wove paper
signed later: 'Edv Munch 1913'
inscribed '2dn Tilstand'
MM G 20–4; W. 22

8 *Self-Portrait* 1895
lithograph
46.0 x 32.0
printed on wove paper, signed in pencil:
'E Munch'
MM G 192–17; W. 37

9 *The Scream* 1895
lithograph
35.5 x 25.4
shown in Glasgow only
MM G 195–3; W. 38

Angst, 1896, woodcut (detail)

Fig. 21 The Munch Museum, Tøyengata, Oslo

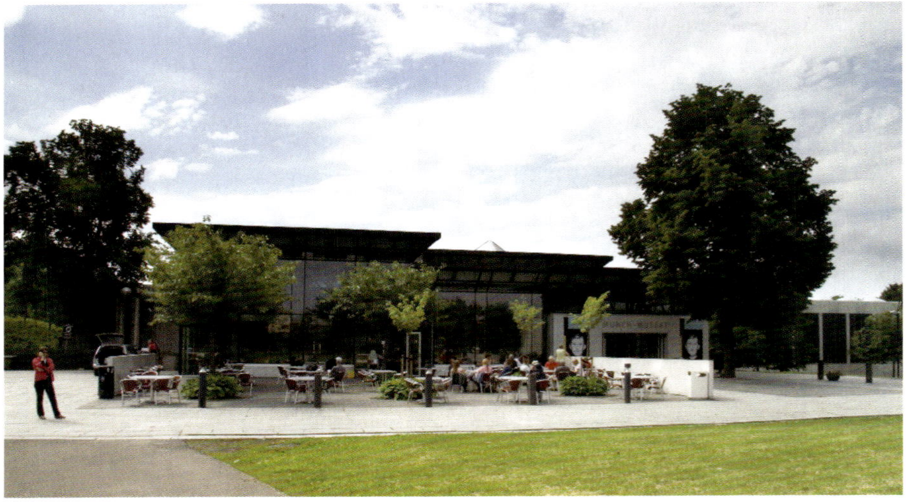

10 *Madonna* 1895/1902
lithograph
60.5 x 44.2
printed on china paper, in blue, red and grey-green, signed 'E Munch'
MM G 194–41; W. 39

11 *Vampire II* 1895
lithograph
36.5 x 46.5
printed in red and black on china paper and washed with grey watercolour, signed in pencil 'Edv Munch'
MM G 567-82; W. 41

12 *Stanislaw Przybyszewski* 1895
lithograph
54.0 x 44.0
MM G 231-10; W. 45

13 *Death in the Sickroom* 1896
lithograph
40.0 x 55.0
signed and dated 'E Munch 96'
MM G 215–3; W. 65

14 *August Strindberg* 1896
lithograph
51.0 x 36.7
early state with the ornamental name 'STIND-BERG' misspelled
MM G 219a–1; W. 66 I/V

15 *Jealousy I* 1896
lithograph
33.0 x 46.0
printed on wove paper, signed in pencil 'Edv Munch'
MM G 201–19; W. 68

16 *The Sick Child I* 1896
lithograph
43.0 x 56.0
printed in grey-blue and two red inks on wove paper, signed 'E Munch'
MM G 203–20; W. 72

17 *Attraction I* 1896
lithograph
47.2 x 35.5
printed on china paper, signed in pencil 'E Munch'
MM G 207-4; W. 75

18 *Separation II* 1896
lithograph
41.5 x 62.5
printed in blue ink on Japanese paper
MM G 210–19; W. 78

19 *On the Waves of Love* 1896
lithograph
39.7 x 50.2
MM G 213–6; W. 81

20 *Moonlight I* 1896
woodcut
47.0 x 48.5
printed in colours from three blocks on China paper, signed on the reverse
MM G 570–19; W. 90

21 *Evening. Melancholy I* 1896
woodcut
38.7 x 45.5
printed on Japan paper and inscribed by Munch: 'Probe für neue Auflage 1914'
MM G 571–6; W. 91

22 *Angst* 1896
woodcut
46.0 x 37.3
printed in black on Japan paper
signed 'Edv Munch'
MM G 568-3; W. 93

23 *Stéphane Mallarmé* 1897
lithograph
52.5 x 30.0
printed on Japan paper
MM G 221-5; W. 99

24 *In the Man's Brain* 1897
woodcut
37.1 x 55.7
printed in red on brownish paper
signed in pencil 'E. Munch'
Hunterian Art Gallery, GLAHA 17985. W. 110

25 *Melancholy II* 1898
woodcut
33.5 x 42.5
MM G 588–4; W. 132

26 *Two Women on the Shore* 1898
woodcut
45.5 x 51.0
MM G 589–13; W. 133

27 *Ashes II* 1899
lithograph
35.5 x 45.4
printed on wove paper
MM G 236–23; W. 146

28 *Woman's Head against the Shore* 1899
woodcut
47.0 x 40.5
printed on Japan paper
MM G 597-37; W. 152

29 *Two Human Beings. The Lonely Ones* 1899
woodcut
39.6 x 54.0
MM G 601-19; W 157

30 *Woman with Red Hair and Green Eyes. The Sin* 1902
lithograph
70.0 x 39.9
printed in yellow, red and blue on wove paper
MM G 241–7; W. 198 V/V

31 *Henrik Ibsen at the Grand Café* 1902
lithograph
43.4 x 59.0
printed on simili-Japan paper
MM G 244–11; W. 200

32 *Melancholy III* 1902
woodcut
38.5 x 45.5
printed by the artist on wove paper
signed 'E Munch'
MM G 606–32; W. 203

33 *The Kiss IV* 1902
woodcut
47.0 x 48.0
printed by the artist, signed 'E Munch' and inscribed 'Selv trykk'
MM G 580–8; W. 204

34 *Violin Concert* 1903
lithograph
48.0 x 56.0
printed by Lasally, Berlin on Japan paper
MM G 25417; W. 243

35 *Salome* 1903
lithograph
40.0 x 30.5
printed on simili-Japan paper
signed 'Edv Munch'
MM G 256–16; W. 245

36 *Friedrich Nietzsche* 1906
lithograph
62.0 x 46.5
printed on wove paper
MM G 263–3; W. 286

37 *Young Women on the Beach II* 1907
drypoint
11.0 x 17.2
printed by Felsing, signed in pencil
MM G 124–1; W. 292

38 *Moonlight by the Sea* 1912
woodcut
18.6 x 25.3
printed by the artist
MM G 630–10; W. 419

39 *Young Couple in a Spruce Forest* 1915
woodcut
32.5 x 58.5
MM G 642–16; W. 540

40 *The Girls on the Bridge* 1918
woodcut and lithograph
49.6 x 42.9
MM G 647–30; W. 628

41 *Self-portrait with Bottle of Wine* 1930
lithograph
42.0 x 51.5
MM G 492–3; W. 712

Select Bibliography

About Munch

Reinhold Heller, *Munch, His Life and Work* (London: John Murray, 1984)

J.P. Hodin, *Edvard Munch* (London: Thames & Hudson, 1972)

Sue Prideaux, *Edvard Munch* (London: Yale University Press, 2005)

General Books and Exhibition Catalogues

Frances Carey, *Modern Scandinavian Prints* (London: British Museum Publications, 1997)

Arne Eggum, Gerd Woll and Marit Lande, *Munch at the Munch Museum, Oslo* (London: Scala, 1998)

Carla Lathe, *Edvard Munch and his Literary Associates* (Norwich: University of East Anglia Library, 1979)

Iris Müller-Westermann, *Munch by Himself* (London: Royal Academy Books, 2005)

Peter Selz, *German Expressionist Painting* (Berkeley: University of California Press, 1957)

Gustav Shiefler, *Meine Graphiksammlung* (Hamburg, Ergänzt und Herausgegeben von Gerhard Schack, Christians Verlag, 1974)

About Munch's Prints

Sigrid Achenbach, *Edvard Munch, Die Graphik im Berliner Kupferstichkabinett* (Berlin: G+H Verlag, 2003)

Arne Eggum and Gerd Woll, *Die Brücke – Edvard Munch*, exhibition catalogue (Oslo: Munch Museum, 1978)

Edvard Munch/Gustav Schiefler: Briefwechsel, 2 Vols., Hamburg, Verein für Hamburgische Kulturgeschichte, 1987

Elizabeth Prelinger, *Edvard Munch Master Printmaker* (New York: W.W. Norton and Co., 1983)

Bente Torjusen, 'The Mirror' in Robert Rosenblum, Arne Eggum et al., *Edvard Munch: Images & Symbols* (Washington, D. C.: National Gallery of Art, 1978)

Gerd Woll, *Edvard Munch, 1895, First Year as a Graphic Artist* (Oslo: Munch Museum, 1995)

Gerd Woll, *Edvard Munch: The Complete Graphic Works* (New York: Harry Abrams, 2001)

Index